Where I Come From

Tales from the Pineywoods

Curt Iles

Creekbank Stories

Dedication

Dedicated to my great-great aunt, Louise Wagnon

I never knew my Aunt Lou but have always felt a soul-kinship with her. Like me, she loved Dry Creek, our Old House, Crooked Bayou Swamp, and the Louisiana Pineywoods. I hope readers of *Where I Come From* will discover the timeless places and people Aunt Lou loved.

Also by Curt Iles

Stories from the Creekbank

The Old House

Wind in the Pines

Hearts Across the Water

Deep Roots

The Mockingbird's Midnight Song

Christmas Jelly

The Wayfaring Stranger

A Good Place

As the Crow Flies

A Spent Bullet

Trampled Grass

Uncle Sam: A Horse's Tale

Where I Come From

Available on Amazon as a paperback and Kindle ebook.

Contact

www.creekbank.net

creekbank.stories@gmail.com

Facebook: @TheCreekTribe

Cover design by Matheus Alves

Cover photo: Clayton Iles Road, Dry Creek, LA

First Edition 2024 Published by Creekbank Stories

Library of Congress Number 2024927657

Manufactured in the United States of America

ISBN 978-0-9705236-6-2   Paperback

ISBN 978-0-9826492-0-6 Hardcover

ISBN 978-0-9826492-3-7 e-book

Contents

Prologue: Patterans

Patterans: "Signs, usually stacked crossed twigs, left along a road by the Roma (Gypsy) people to guide followers."

I like the word. *Patteran.*

Where I Come From is my attempt to leave some patterans for you.

I like what the word patteran encompasses: a journey, maybe even an adventure. I believe most Americans have a tiny tinge of that Roma or Gypsy in our blood. It's called wanderlust.

The English author Rudyard Kipling wrote about it in his poem, "The Gypsy Trail,"

"Ever the world over, lass

Ever the trail holds true,

Over the world and under the world,

And back at the last to you.

Both to the road again,

Follow the *patteran*."

I'd like you to consider *Where I Come From* as your patteran.

This big-hearted book contains stories made from stacks of sticks

and twine and held together by Spanish moss.

I've left a long line of patterans along the winding path.

I hope you find them and that they make your journey more joyous.

Please remember that I didn't build most of these patterans.

I discovered them and tidied them up to ensure that the new traveler could find their way.

I invite you on this Journey as a fellow sojourner, maybe even as a gypsy, because most of us have

that hidden heart-room housing a gypsy soul.

"Let's go over the world and under the world

and back at last to you."

Curt Iles

Dry Creek/Alexandria, Louisiana

Chapter 1

Big-Hearted People

"Tell me who you are, and I'll tell you where you're from."

—Wallace Stegner

I was born in Louisiana when dinosaurs still roamed the earth.

Yes, I'm a Louisiana writer, and I've been around.

The experts say, "Write about what you know." So that's what I do.

I know Louisiana, and more importantly, I love Louisiana.

I write about Louisiana because I know it. I've lived here all my life, and my roots go deep. My people began arriving here in the early nineteenth century, and we've been here ever since.

In spite of my state's many quirks and flaws, I write from the heart of a deep love of its people and their fascinating stories. Everyone's got one if we take the time to stop and listen.

My love of Louisiana overflows in my writing as I choose to share stories about our good, caring people, unique culture, and outdoor beauty. Someone else can write about our shortcomings.

I'm often asked, "What is it you like best about Louisiana?"

That's easy: "How our people are big-hearted."

Big-hearted.

We're a state of big-hearted people. In Where I Come From, you'll meet many of them.

I believe you'll fall in love with them just as I have.

We also have vast expanses of big-hearted places as we make some memorable field trips.

We Louisianians can also poke fun at ourselves and others. A few years ago, LSU played Ohio State for the national championship. A Tiger fan held up a sign: Faster players, better food, prettier women.

Let me clarify this. I don't write about the part of Louisiana most readers and tourists know.

I write about the Pineywoods.

Don't get me wrong. I love the diversity of our state, with its rice paddies, canefields, New Orleans, Cajun culture, and expansive swamps; what other state could hold Mamou, Flatwoods, Tickfaw, and New Orleans in the same bowl of gumbo?

We're the only state "The Father of Waters" chooses to pass through on its way to the Gulf. I'll put our river, the Mississippi, against any of the great rivers of the world.

However, my calling isn't to write about the well-known parts of our state. I write about the overlooked and still undiscovered western spine of Louisiana, known as No Man's Land. My people come from this isolated forested area adjacent to the Texas border.

In earlier history, No Man's Land was known as the Neutral Territory, Neutral Strip, and my personal favorite, the Outlaw Strip.

The strip got its name from the fact that anyone running from the law in Spanish Texas or French Louisiana could find a safe haven in the Outlaw Strip. This reputation continued even after the United States took ownership.

So, remember when I brag about my ancestors arriving early in the Neutral Territory, you can surmise that some of them were running from something or someone back East.

My ancestors chose to settle in this specific area of No Man's Land, known as the Pineywoods. It's a band of pines stretching across the belt line of Louisana. My hometown of Dry Creek sits dead center in those pines.

As I said, it's where my people come from.

Let's see if I can untangle this. I'm a Southern writer who lives in Louisiana's Pineywoods and No Man's Land.

That's a mouthful, but it aptly describes where I come from.

It's who I am.

You'll learn more about these environs I come from throughout Where I Come From.

I realized a long time ago that I'm a storyteller, and my stories radiate out from my hometown in Dry Creek, Louisiana.

We'll end up at the dead end of Clayton Iles Road and sit on the dogtrot porch of the nearly two-century-old log cabin my family calls the Old House.

I look forward to sharing these stories and places with you, they and the people around them who have shaped my life.

I'm in a good season of life to write this book and share its stories. They match up with my life philosophy:

Stay curious.

Be amazed.

Share moving stories.

These sixty-six chapters moved me deeply as I wrote them, sometimes to laughter, often to tears.

No tears in the writer, No tears in the reader.

I believe they'll move you, too.

This is not only a good season for this book but also a good quarter. I've come to realize I'm in the last quarter of my life.

I'm nearly seventy. Don't worry; I've got too many books in my soul to go anywhere yet. Besides, that's out of my control, so I plan to write until they pry the pen from my cold, dead hands.

This book is about seasons, quarters, and journeys.

I've come to view life as a journey on a path that twists and turns, climbs steeply through rugged terrain, and crosses level land with peaceful grasslands. Life is filled with both difficulty and joy.

You'll find these "journey" words peppered throughout Where I Come From, path, road, trail, sojourner, traveler, hiker, gypsy, vagabond, and pilgrim.

So, join me on this remarkable, memorable journey.

On this trek, you'll meet many unforgettable people with big souls. Folks have so many stories to tell if you take the time to listen and then write them down.

If you've read my previous thirteen books, you know that everything I write is underpinned by my love of nature and the amazing outdoors. Those lessons are everywhere if we only slow down and look around.

My stories reveal the words and ideas I value most as a lifelong learner, such as my seven words to live by: perseverance, relationships, influence, kindness, passion, and stewardship. If you read carefully, you'll find these words woven into the tapestry of Where I Come From.

I also choose to see the best in others. I live by the words I read on a handwritten sign in an African refugee camp, "If you like people, people will like you."

I cannot add to that. It's worked well for me so far.

Finally, you'll read about my spiritual journey, which is the bedrock of my life, and my stories. My favorite review is, "Your stories are spiritual without being preachy."

I hope you find this to be true as you read. I see God's fingerprints all around us. I hope Where I Come From reveals those prints to you.

Let's go. It's time to visit a majestic pine called "The Seed Tree."

Chapter 2

The Seed Tree

"Going down South to the land of the pines . . . "

—"Wagon Wheel"

Old Crow Medicine Show

I've been studying a majestic Loblolly pine for over thirty years. It's located along LA Hwy 113 after crossing the Calcasieu River and entering Louisiana's No Man.

This pine first caught my eye because it was the lone tree in the middle of a large pasture.

I've driven Highway 113 all of my life. It connects my boyhood home of Dry Creek to the towns of Pineville, where I attended Louisiana College, and Alexandria, where I now live. For years, cattle grazing the pasture, as well as periodic bush hogging, prevented tree growth.

Except for my big pine.

Several decades ago, the field was allowed to go fallow.

No more grazing.

No more bush hogging.

Before long, a thick grove of young pines sprouted up around the big loblolly. These saplings hadn't been planted but come up as "volunteers." Foresters refer to them as "feral trees."

Over time, the big pine was encircled by a thick cover of young pines. That's when I started calling the tall pine a Seed Tree.

There is a story about the origin of the term seed tree.

When the first settlers arrived in western Louisiana, huge virgin longleaf pine forests populated No Man's Land. That changed at the end of the 19th Century when speculators and northern timber companies gobbled up the land. They built temporary sawmills and cut all of the virgin pine forests. The timber people had a cut-out/get-out policy, leaving nothing behind but miles of pine stumps.

However, sawyers periodically left a solitary longleaf pine as a "seed tree." This allowed the seed tree, or "mother tree," to spread its seeds and replenish the area. From these tall trees, fluttering seeds from the large cones resulted in young volunteer pines.

My big loblolly pine on 113 is a seed tree. I also call it a mother tree.

As the years have rolled on, the surrounding volunteer pines have grown tall against the backdrop of my large tree. These young pines have nearly obscured my Seed Tree. Over time, it'll be hard to distinguish where it stands. A thick grove of children's trees will have taken its place.

Soon, I won't see my Seed Tree on my drive to Dry Creek. We've been friends for over thirty years, and I've watched it faithfully guard this pasture. Then, I'll never see it again.

I don't feel sorry for the seed tree; It's done its appointed job: carrying on the legacy of loblolly pines in that field. Its family will respectfully surround it for the remainder of its days.

You cannot ask for anything better than that.

***

The Seed Tree and my nearing the age of seventy make me think about legacy.

I believe legacy is not only about after you die; it's also about now. You and I are building a legacy around us now.

You don't have to die to have a legacy. You are building a legacy as you live.

Legacy is often defined as "What you leave behind and who you leave it to." However, legacy is much more than property lines, heirship, wills, and your mother's fine china.

Legacy is what you pass on from heart to heart. It cannot be seen or felt, but its presence is always evident. It involves making memories, and those memories don't have to be significant. These memories can be made in so many ways, but they include hands, words, and hearts that touch and bond.

As I consider my lasting legacy, I wonder, "What will I be remembered for and by whom? "

Even though I've written a dozen books and gained a smidgen of notoriety, my writing will not be my true legacy.

It will be my family.

That grove of trees surrounded me. Family.

DeDe and I have been blessed with three adult sons and nine precious grandchildren. They are my most significant legacy at this season of my life, and I want to pour my life into theirs at every opportunity.

You see, I understand the influence of grandparents. I'm the product of four grandparents who loved me unconditionally and left a legacy I've tried to pass on.

When we returned to America in 2015 after our three years in Africa, everyone expected we'd move back to Dry Creek and build a house down Clayton Iles Road.

My wife DeDe, who is always ahead of me, said, "We should move to Alexandria. It's where our grandchildren are." She's more insightful than me, and as usual, she was right.

I joke with my Dry Creek friends that I've been exiled to Alexandria, but that's not true. I'm here because this is where my young pines are growing.

I'm here to see ball games, dance recitals, taekwondo exhibitions, baptisms, church programs, etc. You name it, we're there.

I also get to be with my grandchildren in their everyday lives.

I miss the woods of my home place, but I'm surrounded by young trees that really matter, and they grow up so fast. I have no time to waste.

One of my friends back home asked, "Curt, why in the world would you move away from Dry Creek to Alexandria?"

I shrugged. "There are nine reasons, and they are named Noah, Jack, Jude, Sydney, Luke, Emma, Maggie, Ellen, and Eliza."

Don't feel sorry for me. I get my weekly Dry Creek fix when I visit my mom and walk on my land. In fact, my stationary states, "Curt Iles Dry Creek, LA/Alexandria, LA."

I have dual citizenship.

***

My life statement has changed very little over the past twenty years, "I want to be a man God can use, an encourager, and respected by those who know me best."

My legacy, my dream, and my prayer are to be the kind of man who lives worthy of my family's respect and love. I want to pass this legacy on to the generations I'll never know—a legacy of the things that matter.

A legacy of the heart. A legacy to future stands of pines I'll never know. I want to remember these life lessons from a stately loblolly pine at the eastern edge of Louisiana's No Man's Land.

My wish and prayer for you is that you'll be surrounded by your young pines and relentlessly pour your life into them. Don't forget you can build a legacy even if your young pines are far away or not from your specific forest.

It's worth it.

It's worth it all.

Chapter 3

The Old House

"As a man thinketh in his heart, so is he."

—*Proverbs 23:7*

It's located at *30.6331 N 93.0632 W.*

You'll find it at the dead end of Clayton Iles Road in Dry Creek, Louisiana.

It's what my family calls the Old House.

It's where I call home.

I've always dreaded the call, but I knew it'd happen one day. My sister's message was short, "A tree fell on the Old House last night during the storm."

Before we discuss the fallen tree and its damage, I should explain the Old House and its connection to my family.

My great-great-grandparents, John and Sarah Wagnon, built the original log portion about 1890. As typical of house styles of that period, the Old House is a dogtrot-style house with porches on every side and three chimneys. Four generations of my clan have lived here, each building additional rooms.

As a child, we lived here while my father built the nearby house I grew up in.

The Old House was a solid part of my upbringing. It was filled with a host of great-grandparents, grandparents, uncles, aunts, cousins, lazy dogs, music, coffee, stories, and lots of love.

It's been empty since 1970, but the house's unique place in my life hasn't diminished. I've written most of my first thirteen books on its porch or in front of a roaring fire. Many nights, I've sat in total silence and darkness, awaiting the lonely call of an owl.

It's a big part of who I am.

Four massive ancient trees surround the Old House. I'd always feared one would fall and destroy the house.

One is a gnarled leaning live oak complete with a rope swing used by three generations of Iles kids.

Two red cedars stand guard in the front yard. My great-grandmother remembered the cedars as saplings from her childhood. Most early homesteads in the Pineywoods had a red cedar in the yard, and it was usually the first tree planted. You can learn more about these classic cedars in Chapter 19.

The fourth tree by the Old House is a tall, mature pecan. It butts up against the back porch on the south side. The pecan is the tree that's always worried me. Pecan trees tend to drop large limbs and crash down.

Over the years I've talked to that pecan tree, requesting it to fall south instead of north. Don't laugh about talking to trees. Like dogs, they listen well and never argue.

However, this old pecan didn't listen. During last night's storm, it came crashing down northward on the roof.

It could have been much worse. One of the cedars caught its top and lessened the damage. Sections of the tin roof buckled; rafters and supports were broken under the trunk's weight.

A tree service removed the tree and tarped the roof. When lifted by a crane, the main section of the pecan trunk weighed five thousand pounds.

What really caught my attention was the stump: It was hollow. All these years, this stately pecan tree had been hollow inside. Heart rot brought it down, revealing its inner weakness.

Our series of hurricanes and storms, beginning with Katrina, left a lasting impression on SW Louisiana. It often takes years to rebuild a community. I'm not sure a person's heart-soul ever fully recovers.

During the aftermath of these storms, I learned an enduring lesson: *Storms don't build character. They reveal it.*

Hurricane survivors came from every walk of life. Most showed a core of character by helping in any way they could. These folks opened their homes and hearts.

Sadly, others took advantage of suffering folks, only looking out for themselves.

Good people became better, while others revealed their worst side.

The storms revealed character. They showed what was inside.

We all experience storms. We're either in a storm, coming out of one, or headed to one.

Storms show what we're made of.

They *reveal*.

* * *

Even in this present season of my life, I want to grow in *heartiness*. My heart needs a daily personal relationship with God. It changes and stretches my soul.

I recommend Him with all of my *heart*.

That's a good lesson from the heart of an ancient pecan tree.

As a young man, I wrote a poem about how I felt about the Old House:

The Old House at the End of the Road

If it's possible to love a house like a person

Then the Lord knows I love this old house.

It's a place that reminds me of family

And the things in life that mean the most.

It's the place I come back to when I'm lonely

Or it seems I've lost my way.

Somewhere where I always feel welcome,

And can sit down and think for a while.

This old house is more than boards and nails,

Because it tells me of our past.

As I walk through it, I'm reminded

The special people in our lives never last.

But though they're gone, I will remember

And they'll live inside of me.

This old house reminds me of who I am

And everything I want to be."

Chapter 4

The Eighth of January

It's January 8, and it's not just any ordinary day.

Two songs explain why:

"The Eighth of January" is a fast-paced fiddle song. My great-grandmother, Theodosia Iles, was the Beauregard Parish Fair fiddle champion for most of her adult life, and she *owned* "The 8th of January."

Years later, one of her younger competitors told me, "Son, when your grandmother started swaying and doing a little two-step as she played 'The Eighth of January,' none of us had a chance."

You're reading this and saying, "I've never *heard* of a song called 'The 8th of January.'"

Yes, you probably have.

The fiddle tune commemorates the defeat of the British at the Battle of New Orleans on January 8, 1815. Colonel Andrew Jackson and a motley army routed the British that day. It's the last time shots were fired between our English cousins and America.

We've been rock-solid allies through thick and thin since. However, the Southerner in me relishes the thought of those red-coated professional soldiers getting their cans kicked by an assortment of volunteers, pirates, and ruffians.

If you've ever heard the "Eighth of January" and its rollicking upbeat style, you can nearly "hear" the rout taking place as the stanza takes off at a gallop.

An Arkansas history teacher, Jimmy Driftwood, composed ballads to help his students learn American History. He wrote a song *about* the Battle of New Orleans and put it to the tune of our fiddle song, "The Eighth of January."

The first lines are memorable.

> *"In 1814, we took a little trip*
>
> *Along with Colonel Jackson*
>
> *Down the mighty Missipp.*
>
> *We took a little bacon, and we took a little beans*
>
> *And we fought the bloody British in the town of New Orleans."*

Most Americans have heard "The Battle of New Orleans." They recognize the tune, having sung it, whistled it, and hummed it. Johnny Horton's 1959 version became that year's biggest country hit and has had an enduring shelf life.

As a child, I wore out the 45-rpm Horton record on my parents' phonograph. I can still hear the drums and marching in the background.

My favorite part of the fiddle tune is when the "Eighth of January" switches keys and goes off on a wild ride. Jimmy Driftwood chose that section to insert my favorite lyrics of the song:

"Wellll, they ran through the briars

And they ran through the brambles

And they ran through the bushes where a rabbit couldn't go.

Ran so fast that the hounds couldn't catch 'em

Down the Mississippi to the Gulf of Mexico."

I'm an old man now, but my six-year-old mind still sees the bloody British running for their lives "Down the Mississippi to the Gulf of Mexico."

So happy Eighth of January to you. It's not an American holiday, but it could be.

Maybe it should be.

Happy 8th of January to my friends and readers scattered across the world.

From Theodosia Iles's great-grandson, Curt.

Historical tidbit: The Battle of New Orleans, which took place on January 8, 1815, was fought after the warring parties had signed a peace treaty.

Chapter 5

Prof. Cavanaugh's Best Lecture

T eacher. There's no higher calling. Few professions can influence more than a dedicated, caring teacher.

The best teacher I ever had was Charles Cavanaugh.

This is his story.

I stood nervously in the hallway outside the Louisiana College biology department's second-floor office, waiting to see Professor Cavanaugh. I'd been standing here for several minutes, my chemistry book under one arm and a class drop sheet in the other.

Professor Charles J. Cavanaugh was a Louisiana College institution. "Prof." as he was affectionately known, had taught biology for over thirty years. He was the most beloved and respected teacher at Louisiana College. At first glance, he seemed to be an unassuming and ordinary man. However, on my first day of biology class, when he strode to the podium and began lecturing without any notes, it was apparent I was in the presence of greatness. He was a master teacher who blended a serious love of teaching with a kind smile and a sharp sense of humor.

Prof. Cavanaugh taught both of my first-year biology courses. Without a doubt, he was the most awe-inspiring teacher I'd ever encountered. Never once in those two semesters did I see him use any notes—everything came from his memory and years of experience.

His unique teaching method made the material seem to come alive. Students in his classes never came in late or talked during the lectures. To be in his lectures was to be in the presence of a master at work.

He was so admired and respected at Louisiana College that the school renamed the Science and Math Building "Cavanaugh Hall" even though he was still an active teacher. He retired after teaching for 32 years.

So, I was nervous as I stood outside the office door of this legend. I was here out of sheer desperation. The previous year, I selected science education as my major, mainly due to the powerful influence of Prof. Cavanaugh's biology teaching.

However, during my trek toward becoming a science teacher, I ran into a seemingly insurmountable obstacle—it was called *Chemistry 105*. Being from a rural school, my chemistry background was pretty weak. In fact, after two weeks of class, they'd covered everything I knew plus a heck of a lot I didn't. I desperately found myself drowning in a raging sea of formulas, equations, and complex problems. I felt distraught, discouraged, and hopeless.

I felt confused and lost, realizing I probably could not pass this course—not just this semester, but most likely ever. I saw my dream of teaching science going down the drain. With resignation, I went by the registrar's office and picked up a drop slip. I planned to take the test tomorrow, and after I failed it, drop the chemistry class.

After picking up the drop slip, I impulsively went to Cavanaugh Hall and decided to see Prof. Cavanaugh before heading back to my dorm to lick my wounds.

So, I stood peering in the window of his office, watching him walking back and forth, gathering papers. My courage melted, and I turned to leave. I told myself he probably wouldn't even remember me from last year's classes. Just then, Prof Cavanaugh came out the door.

Impulsively, I blurted out in desperation, "Could I talk to you?"

Prof. Cavanaugh, carrying an armload of papers, smiled, "Sure."

I began my tale of woe to this kindly scholar. I shared how I felt it was God's will for me to become a science teacher. However, with my inability to grasp chemistry, I saw no course but to drop the class and leave behind my dream of teaching science.

Before I could continue, he interrupted me. His smile tightened as he firmly said, "God's will? Son, I'll tell you what God's will is for you—get in there, work, and pass chemistry. That's what God's will is for you!"

He didn't say it unkindly but said it with definite conviction. His face had turned slightly red as he issued this challenge to me.

I really don't know if he said anything else because I was in such shock. I'd come for encouragement from this great man and instead had received a brief, brisk, and clear lecture. Prof. Cavanaugh turned and strode down the hallway, leaving me in the wake of the words he'd just spoken. I felt about two inches tall, and it was as if my own grandpa had just given me a stern lecture.

Well, I studied chemistry hard that night. The next day, I took the test, determined to do my best. Miraculously, I passed it! Well, I passed it with the lowest possible D, but much to my shock, I had passed this test.

However, the greatest miracle was what happened inside me. That very day, I decided that nothing was going to stop me from achieving my goal of teaching. Prof Cavanaugh's challenge in the hallway lit the fire of determination in me. I was going to pass this course or die trying.

One day, a month or so later, in chemistry lab, my teacher, Dr. Dennis Watson, called me to the side and, as he eyed me suspiciously, said, "Iles, what happened to you?"

I believe he thought I'd either had a brain transplant or was a very crafty cheater.

The fact that I eventually earned an A in both the lecture and lab was no great reflection on me; instead, it was a tribute to the fire Prof. Cavanaugh's speech lit in me. His "lecture" in the hallway of the building bearing his name taught me this spiritual truth, which is so essential to grasp:

Most of the time, God's will is much simpler than we choose to make it. It can usually be summed up this way—*Do your best where you are, bloom where you are planted . . . and don't quit.*

It's been a lifetime since Prof. Cavanaugh taught me. I've probably forgotten most of the biology knowledge he taught. I'm pretty rusty on mitosis, DNA models, and cell structure. However, his lecture in the hallway still reverberates in my heart. When I've found myself in tough times, as we all do throughout life, I've taken solace in the words of this wise old Professor who reminded me of the importance of perseverance and hard work.

Yes, I did go on to teach both biology and chemistry. What a great time I had teaching young students about the wonders of science.

Sometimes, during the year, in my senior chemistry classes, I would open my worn college chemistry book and take out a faded, yellowed, dog-eared blank drop slip and share this story. Once again, I was reminded, even as I told them, that in life, we all face times when it seems hopeless and we feel lost and confused.

However, that is always the exact time to buckle down, work hard, and find God's will by simply doing our best.

"Yes, God's will—most often—is simply doing the best we can right where we are."

Once, Professor Cavanaugh told a group of new teachers, "Good teaching is leadership. If you seriously teach your best and show your students you really care about them, one day those students may rise and call you blessed."

* * *

I'd be remiss not to mention Prof.'s wife and life partner, Eloise Gill Cavanaugh. This classic couple shared a common heritage with my family as early pioneers who settled in No Man's Land before the Civil War.

They came from the rich rural soil of Vernon Parish and together planted a lifetime of good seeds that are still affecting generations. They made a great team and will always be cherished by those of us who knew them.

I have a history of the Cavanaugh and Gill families written by Mrs. Eloise, where she notes,

This is the story of your family: men and women of whom you may be proud. May you keep untarnished the good name they have handed down to you.

Chapter 6

Loving Hands

My Aunt Margie Nell had the most beautiful hands in the world. I miss those hands on the piano.

Although I miss Aunt Marge's hands, I miss her heart the most.

Marjorie Nell Iles Walker was my Dad's younger sister. During her lifetime, she was Southwest Louisiana's most renowned pianist. With her unique style and personality, she entertained thousands.

Aunt Margie was a prodigy. My grandmother told me about waking up five-year-old Margie Nell to play the closing hymn at Dry Creek Baptist Church. Aunt Margie had a God-given gift, and she used it well. She was a good steward of that gift.

My Dad, who had a rich baritone voice, was her partner. He and Aunt Margie sang and played all over the state. Neither were shy about sharing their music as only a brother and sister could.

It touched me deeply when Aunt Margie played before and after my Dad's funeral in 2003. It was her personal gift to her singing brother and a precious gift to our family.

Aunt Margie could not only play, but she also had an amazing repertoire and memory and could hardly be stumped.

One of my best memories was a senior adult lunch at Dry Creek Camp. The crowd called out favorites, and she'd pound them out to their delight.

I'd be hard-pressed to describe Aunt Margie's piano style. I guess you had to hear it to describe it. I've often remarked that if I were walking through Grand

Central Station and the P.A. was playing one of her songs, I'd stop and say, "Hey, that's my Aunt Margie Nell."

As her nephew, she always made me feel special, and that's one of the many reasons I loved her dearly.

She'd wink at me as she played my favorite song, "Ashokan Farewell," the haunting theme song from Ken Burns's series, "The Civil War."

She was a performer, chewing on a stick of Wrigley Spearmint gum, smiling and nodding at the audience who were in the palm of her hand, or rather hands.

I loved Aunt Margie for much more than her stunning piano skills. She was the firm grip connecting me to my ancestors from whom she'd inherited her musical ear.

She would regale me for hours (literally) with tales of my grandparents, great-grandparents, and a host of great-uncles and aunts.

I took those stories to heart. Many of them are found sprinkled throughout my books.

Aunt Margie and Uncle Mark possessed what I call Old Southern Hospitality. Regardless of when I showed up unannounced at their door, they dropped everything, and I was greeted as the returning prodigal.

Aunt Margie would heat the pot of coffee that had simmered all day over the pilot light, and we'd drink coffee and visit and visit and visit. Aunt Margie liked to talk as much as she loved the piano, maybe more.

My family still laughs at the art of disentangling from a visit to Aunt Margie.

I'd stand. "Aunt Margie, I'd better get back to Dry Creek."

"Can't you stay a little longer?" As I shuffled out the front door, she was step-by-step in my ear, finishing a story.

As we walked to the truck, she grasped my hand. I carefully closed the cab door and rolled down my window as Aunt Margie kept talking. Often, she'd put those beautiful hands on my door frame as I slowly shifted into reverse to ease away. She'd be waving until I reached the highway.

I'd do anything to grasp those beautiful hands one more time, to hear Aunt Margie using her God-given piano talent to entertain and inspire others.

She was my Aunt Margie, and she was one of a kind.

I miss her and always will.

Chapter 7

John Wooden's Socks

> "It isn't what you do, but how you do it."
>
> —John Wooden

I met John Wooden in 1979 when I was a college senior preparing to become a high school basketball coach. I traveled to Monroe, Louisiana, to hear John Wooden speak at a coaching clinic.

Wooden, who'd retired five years earlier from UCLA, was the most famous basketball coach in America. His teams had won ten national championships, including seven years in a row.

I arrived with my notebook and a desire to learn. The first thing Coach Wooden did surprised me. He sat down on the stage, took off his tennis shoes, and held up a pair of new socks.

"The first thing we did at the year's first practice was to learn how to put socks on." He then proceeded to go over in detail how to fit and wear socks so his players wouldn't get a blister.

Coach Wooden tied his shoes and then launched into a wonderful time of telling stories about his years at UCLA, how he ran practices, and the setup of his famous zone press.

I've forgotten the rest of that coaching clinic, but I've never forgotten the socks. Here was a successful coach who paid attention to the details.

There are numerous theories as to how he put together his championship runs, but anyone who knew Wooden agreed that his attention to detail was a key to his success.

That day, I learned a great lesson: doing the small things right is what separates the best from others.

Thanks, Coach Wooden, for a simple example of how little things matter in the big picture.

In the years since that clinic, I've often thought about those socks. They remind me how attention to detail is a factor in success in anything.

* * *

"Great leaders are ordinary people with extraordinary determination."

-John Wooden

Postscript

John Wooden is still the gold standard by which college basketball coaches are judged. During his tenure as UCLA coach, his teams won ten national championships in twelve years, completed three undefeated seasons, and an unmatched 88-game winning streak. In the midst of this success, he maintained his humility and integrity.

My favorite John Wooden book is *They Call Me Coach*.

Chapter 8

Curt Lies

L et's get this straight from the outset: my name is Curt *Iles*.

My last name is often misspelled. People want to put another s in it as in *Isles*.

Like the Islands. You've probably heard of them: the British Isles. Folks sometimes ask if my family came from the Isles, and I tell them we were exiled for refusing to bow to the King.

My simple last name, Iles, often leads to confusion. Sometimes, folks want to insert a double ss at the end. *Iless* sounds like a snake hissing or a disease.

The worst troublemaker is that a capital I and a lowercase l look identical on a laptop. You can see it in the typesetting of this chapter.

No one wants to be known as Curt *Ills*.

However, I can beat that. A large organization has listed me as *Curt Lies*. I've tried to get it corrected for fourteen years to no avail. I'm resigned to being stuck with that moniker for the remainder of my life. It's impossible to get removed from a vast database. I call it the database of death. You're on it until you die, and they'll keep you subscribed if they find a forwarding address.

I wouldn't be surprised if St. Peter spells it wrong. That's okay as long as he lets me in.

Curt Lies.

Go figure.

* * *

I've told my boys to make sure Curt *Lies* doesn't end up on my headstone. That etching could be as difficult to remove as the database of death.

All of this foolishness has led me to think about lying and the truth.

Truthfulness and lying are habits that are not easily broken. Speaking the truth becomes a habit, as does telling a whopper.

Lying is a habit, just like truthfulness.

What an excellent trait to be known for: *truthfulness.*

A few reminders to self.

Lying and truthfulness are both habits.

If I tell the truth, I never have to remember what I said. If I don't tell the truth, it will eventually come back to bite me right in the butt.

* * *

People have the same trouble with my full name. *Sidney Curt Iles*

I'm proud of my first name. Sidney was the first name of my grandfather and his father.

Because Sidney is my first name, all official correspondence with the government, scammers, and other entities is always addressed to *Sidney C. Iles.*

This worked well until we had a granddaughter named Sydney Iles.

Sydney Kaye Iles.

My granddaughter Sydney is my namesake and she has me wrapped around her little finger.

However, since we both live in Alexandria, it has caused numerous problems for both of us.

I'm Sidney Iles.

She's Sydney Iles.

The library gets us confused.

Our church gets us mixed up.

Our dentist gets us crossways. They'll call me on an appointment, and we go through the dance of getting the right Sydney/Sidney in the dentist's chair. Because I hate going to the dentist, I'm tempted to say, "Oh no, you've got the wrong one."

Sydney K. Iles

Sidney C. Iles

The opportunities for misunderstandings are endless.

* * *

Then I have a middle name that I'm known by,

Sidney *Curt* Iles

It's pretty short: *Curt.*

Webster defines it as "Sparing of words," as in, "Curt was curt."

I've always wanted to write that sentence in a book.

Curt was curt. It kind of rolls off your tongue.

However, a second definition of *curt* is "marked by rude, sharp, shortness."

As in, "In a *curt* voice, he ordered the server to bring him a glass of water."

I don't want to be associated with that second definition, as in, "Curt is *curt.*"

Here's how "Curt" plays out at Whataburger,

"Sir, what name would you like your order under?"

"Curt"

"Sir, is that with a *C or K*?

"Is it *Kirk* or *Curt*?*

"Did you say *Carl* or *Curt,* and is that *Carl* with a C or a K?

A side note: I went to McNeese with a black friend named Charlie. Throughout the semester, he referred to me as "Carl." I paid no mind to it.

Finally, about mid-semester, he said, "Your name's not Carl, is it?"

"No, it's Curt."

He shrugged with a grin, "Well, you know how it is; all of you White people look alike."

I'm still laughing. Charlie Sprott, are you still out there?

By the way, that's Charlie with a C, not K.

Back to the Whataburger checkout,

"Now, Sir, did you say *Cur*? And is that with one r or two?"

I couldn't decide whether to growl or bark.

I've solved the problem at fast-food restaurants.

"Sir, what name do you want your order under?"

"Bob."

No one has ever asked me to pronounce, spell, or repeat it.

Just "Bob."

My grandchildren roll their eyes when "Bob" orders, but it gets the job done.

Writing,

Curt, aka "Bob" Iles, aka "Lies"

P.S. By the way, that's a capital I with a lowercase l.

* * *

One last tidbit: I was married to my sweet wife DeDe over twenty years before my father-in-law, Herbert Terry, stopped calling me "Kirk." I didn't have the heart to correct him, knowing it wouldn't have made a difference anyway.

Chapter 9

Hugh Thompson on Integrity

"Integrity is who you are when no one is looking

and what you will stand up for even if you're standing alone."

—John Maxwell

S ay his name out loud. *Hugh Thompson.*

It's a name worth remembering.

I was recently in Lafayette, Louisiana, and visited Hugh Thompson's grave at Lafayette Memorial Park Cemetery. It's the final resting place of an American hero who should never be forgotten.

Rather than ramble on about what integrity is, I'll tell a story. It's a remarkable true story that won't be easily forgotten.

Hugh Thompson wasn't born in Louisiana, but he's buried here and was an unsung hero on one of America's saddest days of the Vietnam War.

You probably aren't familiar with Hugh Thompson's name or history. Here's his unforgettable story:

On March 16, 1969, Thompson was circling his Army helicopter over the village of My Lai, providing cover for the American troops on patrol. From his vantage point above the palm trees and rice paddies, he watched a terrible sight. The soldiers were shooting unarmed civilians.

Observing a group of women being chased by soldiers, Hugh Thompson made a decision. He landed his helicopter between the fleeing villagers and fellow American soldiers. Climbing out of his helicopter, Thompson instructed his machine gunner to train his weapon on the soldiers and shoot if they continued their slaughter.

Hugh Thompson jumped out of his chopper and angrily confronted the soldiers.

They threatened to shoot him, but he didn't budge. Finally, the troops dispersed, and Thompson gave aid to several wounded young women.

His brave action saved dozens of lives that day, but that's not the end of the story. His actions that day at what came to be called the My Lai Massacre didn't earn Thompson a medal or accolades. He was persecuted for the remainder of his military career.

All for doing what he knew was the right thing.

Thirty years later, Hugh Thompson returned to My Lai with a crew from CBS' *60 Minutes*. He was reunited with several of the villagers he'd saved. When asked on camera why he'd made his heroic decision that day, he shrugged and said, "I knew it was the right thing to do, and I'd always been taught to do the right thing."

That describes integrity. It's doing the right thing.

Whether it's unpopular or not.

Whether it's recognized as right or wrong.

Whether it's rewarded or scorned. That's integrity.

Doing the right thing regardless of what it may cost you.

Integrity remembers that what's popular isn't always right, and what's right isn't always popular.

Like Hugh Thompson, it's a willingness to stand for what's right in the middle of chaos.

It's an inner moral compass that ignores the winds of exterior pressure and performs rightly.

Integrity is doing the right thing regardless of the situation or consequences.

Integrity doesn't develop overnight. It is the product of a series of small, lifelong decisions to do the right thing and hold firm to your beliefs.

Always do the right thing regardless of the circumstances.

Yes, say his name out loud. *Hugh Thompson.*

It's a name worth remembering.

* * *

Integrity is in precious short supply these days.

–Priscilla Shirer

The Forgotten Hero of My Lai by Trent Anger is an excellent biography about Hugh Thompson.

You can learn more about Hugh Thompson's story on YouTube and Google.

Chapter 10

The Night The Old House Came Alive

I leave my mom's home and walk the short distance to the Old House. It's sunset, and our homestead, built in 1892, stands starkly against the background of Crooked Bayou Swamp.

I hurry in from the cold and build a fire in the middle room fireplace, my favorite room, where I spent countless hours with my grandmother.

The Old House is now over thirteen decades old and hasn't been occupied since the 1970s. Despite that, the old lady is in fair shape for her age, but it's been dark, empty, and lonely for many years.

I have an odd thought as I sit by the roaring fire: *Why don't I go through the darkened house and see which lights work?*

I pull the light cords, and every light, including the porch lights, comes on. I go out in the front yard, and I'm amazed. The Old House *is aglow with light.*

The Old House is alive . . . again.

I can't recall the last time I saw it like this. Alive again after all these years of darkness.

I take a chair to the front yard and soak in the eerie time of day when dusk slides into nightfall. This gathering darkness only illuminates the Old House.

As a boy, I recall coming out of the swamp after dark and walking in the general direction of home until I saw the lights of the Old House. I now knew where I was. I was headed home.

I return to my mesmerizing fire, carefully easing onto a rickety cowhide chair as my dog, Bandit, takes his place by the hearth.

I have a vivid imagination. That's where thirteen books and novels will lead you.

What happens next is imagination from deep in my heart. It wasn't real, but it felt like it was:

I hear footsteps on the wooden porch. I step outside to see generations of my family emerging from the dark. They're all healthy and alive again—several walk up from the swamp, smelling of squirrels and Garrett's sweet snuff.

Another shadow appears from the east forty carrying an armload of rich pine kindling. My grandfather, whistling a Jimmy Rodgers's tune, walks by with a bushel of roasting ears.

Headlights appear on the gravel road as other ancestors arrive in old cars with fiddle cases, guitars, and homemade casseroles.

They crowd into the places where I knew them best: in the log room, the old kitchen, and the two bedrooms sharing a double fireplace.

Most congregate on the dogtrot porch, where they tune their instruments. As always, it takes forever. My father, healthy again, stands among them, poised to launch into one of his ballads. My Uncle Clint, standing beside my father, breaks into a grin and winks at me.

The aroma of dark roast Seaport coffee wafts from the kitchen. It's mingled with the laughter of country women working together. The creaking of swinging screen doors fills the air as they come and go.

They're all here. My grandparents, great-grandparents, and a host of uncles, aunts, and cousins surround me.

There are several I don't recognize, but they smile and seem to know me. I realize they're the ancestors of this house I never knew: John and Sarah Wagnon, who built this old house, and their daughter Louise. They lived their entire lives here long before my time.

These are the pioneers who homesteaded these eighty acres, built the log house, cleared the land, and laid the foundation for what the Old House is today.

The foundation they laid was much more than logs and boards. It's a legacy passed down to me and the generations to follow—a legacy of the land, enduring family ties, and love.

Next, in my dream, other cars arrive. They are my sons, their wives, and my nine grandchildren.

They mix and mingle with family members they only knew by name or story.

I think about the old Southern song, 'Will the Circle Be Unbroken?"

Tonight, that circle is complete at the Old House. We're all here.

I'm not sure how long this reunion lasts.

I look up, and the fire has died down. Although the lights are on, the Old House is empty again.

It's just me and Bandit, but I don't feel lonely or sad. I feel a warmth from the legacy of my deep roots in these Pineywoods.

I cover the fire and walk through each room, pulling the switch cords off until the Old House is once again dark.

Before stepping away, I flip the porch light back on — just in case someone is arriving late at the Old House.

At the Old House that sits on the edge of Crooked Bayou swamp.

* * *

Postscript

Was it real? Of course not, but I quietly wept as I sat in front of the fireplace.

I'm teary-eyed now as I type. It may not have been real, but it was special and moved me beyond words.

It won't be the last time in this book where I write:

No tears in the writer, no tears in the reader.

Chapter 11

The Hundred-Foot Line

A fine stand of young slash pine is growing at Dead Man's Curve on the Longville Gravel Pit Road. I've watched this forest grow since it was clear-cut five years ago and then replanted in straight rows of pine seedlings.

Those pines quickly began to poke their heads through the tall grass, soon emerging above the surrounding bushes and scrub trees. In the coming years, they'll link canopies, drop their pine straw, and completely wipe out the other growth in this field.

If a woods fire doesn't kill them first.

I've been inspecting the fire lane plowed around these pines. With winter approaching and its accompanying grass-killing frosts, having good fire lines is essential.

Woods fires break out when a cold front and north wind dry out the ground and grass. Burning the woods is a long tradition among the folks in western Louisiana's "No Man's Land." It began with the early cattlemen and sheepherders burning off the dead grass, believing that new fresh grass was better for their livestock.

Our native longleaf pines can survive most woods fires, but due to their slow growth, longleafs have been replaced by newer species. Louisiana's reforestation in the last eighty years has been accomplished with faster-growing loblolly and slash pines.

The tradeoff is that these species cannot survive a hot woods fire. There's nothing sadder than a field of burnt dead pines, meaning a loss of trees and habitat from fire.

For years, Southwestern Louisiana led the entire state in woods arson. The old settlers still believed it was their right to burn the woods.

Feuds over hunting leases or grudges led to "revenge fires." Sometimes, the fires were set accidentally and spread by a strong wind and low humidity. Regardless of the source, our two most common species of pines are exceptionally vulnerable to fire.

I always worry about fields like the slash pines on Longville Road. Once tall enough, they can withstand most fires. However, for the first five years or more, a hot fire will often destroy an entire stand.

That's why wise forest owners will plow a second inner "hundred-foot line."

This fire break is insurance against the arsonist who tosses matches across the outer fire lane. The plowed lane can stop the fire before it spreads to the entire pine plantation.

It provides insurance for the more significant part of the field.

I see a spiritual component to the hundred-foot line. In our busy lives, we need this guardrail of space and protection for our minds and souls. This fire lane, or margin, gives us boundaries and space to breathe.

It allows us to control the raging fires that can burn in our lives. I know all about that—I've had some hot fires in my own heart—usually self-inflicted.

How do we plow those hundred-foot lines?

Here are two ideas:

Be still.

I love the words of the shepherd David in Psalms 46:10,

"Be still and know that I am God."

These words are both a promise and a commandment. We must take time to be still, get quiet, pray, and meditate.

We must build solitude and silence into our lives and guard a time and place for them.

Get Outdoors.

> "The Bible was written to be read outdoors."
>
> -Wendell Berry

There's something about being out in nature: a clear blue sky, the wind in the pines, an owl's call, and a star-filled winter sky with a fingernail moon.

Get outdoors. Being outside is good for the inside of a man.

Be sure your hundred-foot fire lanes are in order. It's much easier to plow lines than to replant pines.

Chapter 12

Elmer's Hand

"Giving breaks the grip of greed."

—Todd Strain

Elmer Conner had a unique view of asset management.

I can walk to the exact spot where I met him by the coffee pot in the Dry Creek Camp cafeteria. I'd been told that Elmer, an extremely successful contractor in Lake Charles, had a unique philosophy on finances, generosity, and faith.

I wanted to know more. I introduced myself and asked about his foundational beliefs concerning finances, giving, and generosity.

He set his coffee cup down and held up an open palm. "Son, when God begins blessing people with wealth, He's doing it so we can bless others."

Elmer used his free hand as if placing money into his open palm, then clenched his fist. "We tend to close our fists, thinking these resources are ours, not God's.

"There's a two-fold problem with this: first of all, we can't bless others with a tight fist."

Elmer smiled. "Secondly, if we close our fist, God is not able to keep pouring the blessings into our hand."

He opened his hand. "God wants us to live with an open hand."

It was one of the best lessons I've ever heard. It became what I call "Open-Hand Living."

I can attest that Elmer's way of approaching blessings works.

I am forever grateful for that profound story. That's why I'm passing it on.

Thanks, Elmer, for that enduring lesson by the coffee pot. You may be gone, but you still live and influence through your powerful story.

" . . . and through his faith, though he died, he still speaks."

-Hebrews 11:4

During my years of working with men and women like Elmer, who loved Dry Creek Camp, I learned a simple truth: You cannot outgive God.

We are called to be stewards of everything God places in our hands and lives. Stewardship entails holding and taking care of what's been entrusted to us.

We don't own it, but we take care of it seriously.

It's called stewardship.

Stewardship. What a fine word.

Postscript

The story is told of a little girl whose father wanted to teach a lesson on giving. He gave his daughter two one-dollar bills. "Honey, one of these dollars belongs to God; the other is yours to spend as you wish."

The girl was thrilled and hurried, both bills in hand, to the nearest candy store.

Just as she stepped over a storm drain, one of the bills fell from her hand and dropped through the grate.

She rebounded quickly. "Ut-oh, God. That one was yours."

We laugh but sometimes forget that God owns it all.

Chapter 13

The Deer Hunter

I come from a deer-hunting culture and grew up around some of the best deer habitat in the Pineywoods.

I hate to admit this, but I've never been a good deer hunter. I'm not patient enough to sit very long in a cold deer stand, nor am I willing to put in the time to prepare for a successful hunt.

However, I love a good hunting story, and this is definitely one.

There are some people you like the first time you meet them. That was true of Chet, and it was also true of Michael.

I first met Chet in early November when he approached a table of men who meet weekly for breakfast and Bible study. It was the first week of deer season. One of the men said, "Chet, how'd you do?"

Chet smiled. "I got two, and one was a fine eight-point."

"You really enjoy hunting, don't you?"

"I do." Then Chet stopped, and his voice changed. "But . . . what I like best is taking folks hunting who could never kill a deer on their own."

Chet described an apparatus he'd built to aid an immobile person to hunt. He'd built the contraption with knobs and adjustments to sight in the rifle, including a blowing straw that pulls the trigger.

I listened with interest. *I've got to see this thing in action.*

Chet continued. "That's the real joy I get from hunting."

He described a memorable hunt with a younger man, and I realized he was speaking of my friend Michael.

I fell in love with Michael the first time I met him. We worship together, and he is a friend of my son's.

Michael has been confined to a wheelchair all of his life, but that's the *only way* he's confined. He has a college degree, loves God, has a fine sense of humor, and is passionate about his Atlanta Braves.

Chet took Michael deer hunting, and that's the best part of the story.

I'll let Chet tell it:

"We got Michael situated in a stand and showed him how everything worked. The first few opportunities passed without success, but then it happened.

"A good-sized buck came into view on the scope. When the crosshairs settled on the deer, Michael blew a puff, and the buck went down.

"Michael yelled as loudly as I've ever heard a man holler. You could probably hear him all the way into LaSalle Parish. I was standing with his dad, Mickey, and both of us shouted and cried."

Chet glanced around our table, "Guys, now that's *how* I like to hunt."

Chet's story touched me deeply, especially since I know Michael and his family.

You may have a lump in your throat as you read it, too. That's a good thing. That's why stories are so powerful. They move us, sometimes to tears, and that's not a bad thing.

Chapter 14

Earthshine

"There's a full moon on the horizon

And it nearly fills the sky;

Thank you, Lord, you made it right;

You made it right."

—"You Made It Right"

Ozark Mountain Daredevils

P ut it on your calendar: July 20— It's International Moon Day.

It coincides with the anniversary of the Apollo moon landing on Sunday, July 20, 1969.

Dusk

Early Spring

Dry Creek, Louisiana

We sit on logs and chairs huddled around the campfire. All six of us are stuffed with hot dogs washed down with hot chocolate.

It's the special type of evening that March brings to Louisiana: cool, clear, low humidity, and a light breeze. We're sitting around our firepit overlooking the pond.

My 89-year-old mother sits to my right. She's bundled up against the chill with a shawl.

My youngest son, Terry, and his wife, Sara, sit to my left.

Their two daughters, Emma and Eliza, my granddaughters, run up and down a nearby dirt pile. I watch as their headlamps bob up and down in the darkness.

To the west, we watch a red sunset settle over Crooked Bayou Swamp.

It's now the time of evening I love best.

Gradually, my friends begin to appear in the SE sky.

One single star shines in the gathering darkness. It's Sirius, the dog star, the brightest star in the sky. It forms the heart of the constellation Canis Major, the Big Dog.

I nod to Terry. "Can you see Orion yet?" My night eyes aren't as good as they once were.

After a minute, Terry says, "I can see his belt."

Orion is most easily found by the constellation's three-line perfectly aligned bright stars. Known as "The Hunter," it is my favorite winter constellation. He spends the cold months of the year moving across the south sky, his faithful dog Canis at his side.

Momma's not interested in the stars. She's just trying to keep warm. As the girls continue their escapades, Sara begins loading our gear in the back of my truck.

Terry and I sit enjoying the night, the outdoors, and the experience of being together. We've always been comfortable in each other's presence, and today is no exception.

Terry glances over his shoulder. "Daddy, look at the Moon."

A thin fingernail slice of a crescent waxing moon looms over the western tree line. I've always loved this phase as a new Moon continues its march to a full one.

"Look, Terry, it's Earthshine."

Earthshine is the faint, lovely glow on the Moon's unlit portion. It only occurs in the crescent Moon's waxing or waning phase. The dark portion of the Moon (the area unlit by the Sun) seems to glow.

Earthshine is actually the reflection of the Earth's light on the lunar surface.

The sunshine reflected off the Earth illuminates the dark surface of the Moon.

That's quite a mouthful.

Sun to Earth

Earth to Moon

Earthshine.

You'd be wise to sketch it out on a paper napkin.

The dark, invisible part of the Moon glows in a soft gray orb, making its complete shape easy to discern.

Earthshine was historically called "The New Moon in the Old Moon's arms."

I like that description.

Earthshine is not visible under city lights. You have to be in dark-sky country, and Dry Creek is deep within that territory.

An Earthshine Moon needs a dark night to show off.

Tonight, the clouds have kindly stayed away.

Our only satellite, the Moon, is about 233,000 miles away but still amazes me with its phases, hues, and moods.

* * *

Back at the fire, Terry, Sara, Mom, and I sit silently. The comforting fire draws us together, and the fellowship is even warmer than the fire. Mom's ready to get warm, and it's near bedtime for the girls, so everyone loads up and leaves the woods.

Everyone but me. "Y'all go on. I'll make sure the fire is out."

Soon, I'm enveloped in the silence of a Dry Creek night. I watch as the canopy of stars continues their slow trek across the sky.

Two barred owls begin a hooting contest across the swamp. The yip of a coyote breaks the silence.

I stare into the fire. It's one of the healthiest things a man can do. I call it a *Thinking Fire.*

An outdoor fire clears one's head and opens one's heart.

And tonight, my heart is open. Open with emotion.

I think about Earthshine and how unique and rare it is. It's a gift.

I think about my precious mom. She's a strong eighty-nine. She's made me promise to take her to Branson for her 90th birthday, which I hope to fulfill, even if I have to put her on my back.

Recently, I took Momma to Golden Corral, and we both got senior discounts. We both laughed.

I silently thanked God. Few children still have a living parent at my age.

Mom and I have a limited number of campfires left between us. She speaks freely of it. I can't bear to even think about it.

* * *

Then I think about Terry and his family. In the coming months, he'll begin a new job teaching at New Orleans Baptist Seminary.

I'll have future campfires with Emma and Eliza, but they won't be as frequent. I also know from experience how quickly grandchildren go from climbing dirt piles in the dark to their teen years.

The fire has died down. I kick it, and embers fly like fireflies. I'm in no hurry to leave.

The earthshine-reflected Moon sets behind the trees.

I sit for a long time before rising to leave the woods.

I thank God for the blessings of this night.

I thank Him for my family.

. . . and I thank Him for Earthshine.

Chapter 15

Lost at Sea

Today is Veteran's Day. It's a good time to remember Milton Tinsley. He has a simple marker at Hopewell Community Cemetery near DeRidder, Louisiana:

Milton Tinsley

Lost at Sea

That's all—no information about his story or short life.

I learned of Milton Tinsley's story from his sister, Kathleen Tinsley Heard. Mrs. Kathleen gave me Milton's photo and told her brother's story in a quivering voice. It was evident that his life and death still held a tender place in her heart. The following passage contains his sister's recollections, interspersed with reports from surviving American captives and details from the Internet.

Milton Tinsley was twenty-six when the Japanese attacked Pearl Harbor. He enlisted in the United States Merchant Marines and was soon at sea. The Merchant Marines are an overlooked branch of our service. During wartime, merchant marine ships and crews are assigned to the US Navy, providing invaluable service ferrying supplies to war zones.

Milton Tinsley was assigned as a crewman aboard the Texaco-owned SS *Connecticut*. The ship, with a crew of fifty-five, left Port Arthur, Texas, with a load of gasoline and heating oil bound for Cape Town, South Africa.

Five days later, on April 22, 1942, in the South Atlantic Ocean, the *Connecticut* was torpedoed by a German Patrol Torpedo (PT) *Esau*.

The torpedo and resulting fire killed thirty-three crew members. The survivors escaped in life rafts and were picked up by the nearby German merchant raider *Michel*.

Milton Tinsley was one of the twenty-two survivors.

* * *

His sister Kathleen Heard shared this account from the few *Connecticut* survivors who returned to America after the end of the war.

"Milton was wounded in the attack, but what led to his death was his diabetic condition and lack of insulin. The American survivors related how saddened the German sailors were by Milton's death. The Germans gave Milton a proper sailor's service before he was buried at sea."

It's easy to hate an enemy from periscope depth, but it is much different to watch one die slowly under your care.

Buried at sea.

It has a startling jolt to it: Buried at Sea.

* * *

I dug deeper and found more information concerning the final voyage of the *Connecticut* and its survivors:

The other eighteen *Connecticut* survivors, minus Milton, ended up in a Japanese prison camp until the end of the war. Two died under the barbaric conditions of the Japanese POW camps. Only sixteen returned to tell their story.

The wreck of the *Connecticut*, with thirty-three crew members entombed, lies at the bottom of the Atlantic at coordinates 22.58 S 16.05 W.

The German raider *Michel* sank fifteen Allied freighters in 1942. *Connecticut* was the second casualty.

In 1943, the *Michel* was torpedoed by an American submarine off the coast of Japan. All 263 crew members went down with their ship.

. . .

World War II was a terrible and bloody struggle. I'm glad to say the good guys won. Our freedom was preserved at a terrible cost.

That's probably why Milton Tinsley has been on my mind. He died young, at age twenty-six, never to have a family or enjoy a full life. For all practical purposes, his life has been lost to time and memory.

My job this Veteran's Day has been bringing Milton Tinsley back to life.

I hope I've done that with this story.

I hope it makes you pause and remember freedom is never free.

Milton Tinsley

Lost at Sea

Rest in Peace

* * *

"They have no grave but the sea."

Chapter 16

Trade-offs

"Pick a Side."

—Albert Ortis

* * *

"There are two things you should never sell: a dog or a gun."

Life is full of decisions, and each one is a trade-off.

We gain some things while losing others.

There's no shortcut.

We'll win something as we lose something else. Seldom is any decision "a complete win." Every gain means some form of pain and will often mean some loss.

"Trade-off" isn't a four-letter word, but it's important to weigh those trade-offs before deciding.

Making wise decisions. Considering the consequences.

It boils down to this. Will my decision gain more than I lose?

Will this decision lead me closer to my life goals?

Will this result in a closer walk with God?

That's called seeking God's will.

In each season of my life, God seems to work through nudges in my soul, coupled with open and closed doors.

* * *

As usual, I have a story for everything. I'm calling this one "When Two Fools Meet."

The story concerns "Rebel," a prized hunting dog. It was considered the best squirrel-hunting dog in North Louisiana, if not the entire state.

Rebel was so good that a man drove from East Texas and pulled out a wad of $100 bills thick enough to choke a dog.

Pun intended.

The man counted fifty crisp one-hundred-dollar bills on the hood of his truck. "I'm here to buy your dog, and I have $5,000 in cash."

Rebel's owner stood silently for an uncomfortable minute before quietly saying, "Sir, I'm sorry, but this dog ain't for sale."

The Texan pointed at the dog owner's truck and house. "Look, Mister. I can look at your beat-up truck and ramshackle house. You could use $5,000."

The dog owner said emphatically, "Sir, Rebel ain't for sale for no price."

The elderly father of the dog owner was sitting on a nail keg listening to the conversation. He walked up to the two men and shook his head. "It ain't every day that two fools meet. One, a man who would pay $5000 for a dog, and another one who wouldn't sell it for that price."

* * *

Stories like this one are why I love the Louisiana Pineywoods.

Some folks might not understand the joy of watching a dog on the hunt, treeing a cat squirrel, then loudly baying as it claws on the bark of a beech tree. I know the image isn't politically correct, but it's unforgettable.

Some folks might even frown at eating pan-fried squirrel, but I bet they can understand the gist of this story:

Some things are priceless.

Coming from a dog culture, I suspect the dog owner's refusal to sell wasn't about his dog's hunting ability but more about that deep, nearly sacred connection between a man and his dog.

Some readers will scoff at the story, but that means they haven't had a heart-connection with a special dog.

I know. I owned a gifted labrador retriever named Ivory.

Let me rephrase it. *Ivory owned me.*

Ivory was a yellow Lab that belonged to my son Clint. When he left for Louisiana Tech, Ivory became my dog.

She was the best dog I've ever had. One of the joys of my life was watching her retrieve ducks in flooded timber or a marsh pond. A retriever is so much more than just a hunting dog. The sight of her swimming across Bundick Creek with a wood duck in her mouth brought me a deep sense of joy.

It was clearly evident that Ivory was joyful, too.

She was doing what she was born to do.

Would I have sold Ivory for $5,000?

Heck, no. Some things are not for sale at any price. Even after Ivory's retrieving days were over and she limped around on gimpy legs, she was still a special part of our family.

This dog ain't for sale for any price.

I cried like a baby on the day when Dr. White put her down.

* * *

Back to trade-offs and tough decisions.

The best way to resolve a difficult choice is to seek God's guidance, list the pros and cons of the decision, and then make the best, most well-informed choice.

When my sister Colleen was a teen facing a difficult decision, she'd tear out a sheet of notebook paper and draw a vertical line down the page. She made two headings, "Pro" and "Con." This paper chart would help her make trade-off decisions.

Colleen saw a draft of this story and corrected me: *"Curt, it has been a long time since I thought about my 'pro/con' list. "I think because I finally figured out that's not the answer. We can't make decisions on paper but through prayer. Many times, I still replace prayer with worry.*

* * *

I've thought about a Biblical correlation to Sister Colleen's list and prayer. In the Old Testament book of Second Kings, King Hezekiah received a threatening letter from a nearby powerful king.

Hezekiah took the letter from the messengers and read it. Then he went up to the temple of the Lord and spread it out before the Lord.

It still seems like a good plan to me.

Write it down. Lay it out before the Lord.

Pray for God's direction and guidance.

Watch for open doors and nudges.

Pay attention to closed doors. They are often part of God's leading.

* * *

Some trade-offs are "No-Go."

Some decisions are automatic no-decisions.

I describe it as, "Now, why would I want to go and do something stupid like that?"

Sometimes, the best decision is no decision.

Trade-offs or trade-ins are not an option in some decisions.

My cousin Mark Roy was larger than life, exuberant, full of life, love, and a deep commitment to the Lord. He was a character, and I loved him dearly. Anyone who goes by the nickname "Pine Knot" is my kind of man.

His sudden death in 2024 shocked everyone in his hometown of Iowa, Louisiana. Mark and his wife Debbie had raised their family in Iowa. He was a gifted carpenter who built dozens of houses throughout SW Louisiana. He'd lived a full life committed to his family and the Lord.

Although his funeral was sad, it also had a sense of joy—an exuberance like Mark's.

Mark and his wife Debbie have three beautiful daughters. Each of the sons-in-law spoke at the service. Each gave this same story with slight variations.

"I was nervous when I went to ask Mr. Mark for his daughter's hand in marriage. He listened as I made my entreaty.

"After waiting what seemed like an eternity, he said, 'All right, you've got permission to marry her, but remember, this ain't Walmart. We don't take returns.'"

This ain't Walmart, and we don't take returns.

Well said, Cousin Mark.

AKA Cousin Pine Knot.

Some things aren't tradeable or worthy of trade-offs.

* * *

There is never a guarantee otherthat s will consider your trade-off decision as wi

You own it.

You decide it.

No one else can. You make it and live with it.

Additionally, it is not guaranteed that it will seem like a good decision within a year. That's why life is risky and exciting.

I know about trade-offs. In 2012, DeDe and I sold what we had in Dry Creek and went to Africa.

It wasn't easy, but it was wonderful. We knew we were in the center of God's will, and that was a great place to be.

However, it was still a trade-off. We were away for the birth of three grand-daughters and missed many family gatherings. DeDe lost her brother and father while we were in Africa.

When we returned to America in 2015, we faced another crossroads: Where would we live?

Many people, including my family, expected us to move back to Dry Creek and build a house on our family land; DeDe, whom I listen to, said, "We don't need to move back to Dry Creek. Our families are in Alexandria. We need to live in Alexandria. It's where our grandchildren are."

It was a reasonable trade-off. Nothing can balance against being among nine grandchildren weekly.

Sure, I miss the clear night sky and an open horizon to watch a sunset or moonrise.

The calls of the owls and coyotes at night.

I miss being able to build a bonfire wherever and whenever I please.

I miss the quietness at the end of Clayton Iles Road.

For the first time as an adult, I didn't own a tractor. I miss bush hogging, one of life's most therapeutic chores.

I still miss my lifetime Dry Creek Church family, to whom I will always feel close.

However, I like being close enough to Home Depot to make two trips in one day if I wish. I don't have to drive thirty minutes to Walmart or an hour to Texas Roadhouse on a Friday date night.

I've found a new church family that I love deeply.

I will never leave my Dry Creek friends, but living in Alexandria has opened a new circle of friends.

I am a man most blessed.

Trade-Offs

They're part of life.

They're about counting the cost and making a wise decision.

To move ahead, you must necessarily leave something behind.

It may mean turning down $5,000.

It may involve changing continents.

Most of the time, our decisions are mundane, but don't understate these daily decisions. They add up and point us, like a compass, in the direction of our lives.

These are your decisions.

No one else can, or should, make them for you.

It's your call. You own it.

Trade-Offs. It's the story of valuing priceless things.

May it always be so.

Chapter 17

A Falling-Out

I was told this story years ago. It's still one of my favorites.

Two brothers were excellent carpenters and built houses together throughout the hill country near Fredericksburg, Texas.

One day, they had a *falling out,* which resulted in them refusing to speak to each other.

Despite that, they continued building houses together. They knew each other's work from years of building side by side; they could do it without speaking to each other. They talked around each other and, as needed, "sent messages" through co-workers.

They continued building houses together for nearly a decade without speaking a word. And it was all because of that falling-out ten years before. No one knew what their falling-out was over despite the long shelf life of the grudge,

Then, one day, out of the blue, one of the brothers laid down a two-by-four, "You know what I haven't seen in a long time? A chicken snake."

Moments passed as the second brother stood in thought, hammer at his side,

"Come to think of it, I haven't seen one either."

That broke the ice, and the dam burst. The brothers enjoyed each other's company and built many more houses *together* for the rest of their lives.

I guess you could say they buried the hatchet (or the hammer).

A falling-out was repaired.

Falling-outs are much more than disagreements. Disagreements are part of life, but a falling-out results in a broken relationship. There's a stubborn unwillingness to forgive and move on. The longer a falling-out lasts, the more bitter it can become.

Nothing good can come out of bitterness. It's possibly the deadliest of all human emotions.

I've seen fall-outs of all flavors in the Pineywoods, but many have come from several sources: land, money, and dogs.

Sadly, disputes over family land or possessions are most cringe-worthy.

Disagreement over a property line, hurt over the division of inherited land, an argument over who gets Momma's china or Daddy's Browning twelve-gauge pump shotgun.

None of these should happen, but they do. Most fallouts *continue* because of pride. No one is willing to give in and make the first step.

. . .

I want to add a disclaimer. Even if you step up and attempt to reconcile, it doesn't guarantee the other will be open to closure.

It takes one to forget and two to reconcile.

Reconciliation can be messy. Sometimes, despite your sincere effort, you may be rebuffed and seem to make things worse.

However, if you make the first step, call or visit, you will have done your part. It's no longer in your hands. You can go to sleep at night knowing you did your dead-level best to make it right.

* * *

Another story, "Two Sisters," illustrates another falling-out:

Sometimes, it takes a storm to heal a falling-out.

I'd known the two sisters and several generations of their clan. When I heard they had a falling-out, it saddened me. I don't like to see Dry Creek families on the outs. I don't know what they disagreed over. I wonder if, after these years of stony silence, they even remembered what ignited their disagreement. Even sadder, their children also fell out. Two sisters and a line of cousins became estranged. There were no Christmas cards and no family reunions.

One sister lived in Dry Creek, the other an hour away in Lake Charles. It might as well have been a thousand miles. They'd dug in after falling-out, and it seemed destined to last a lifetime.

A storm in 2005 changed all of that. Her name was Hurricane Rita. Rita was Katrina's younger sister, and she struck SW Louisiana about three weeks after her Big Bad Sister Katrina.

I rode out Rita and can attest she was a bad girl, too.

Ahead of Rita, a mandatory evacuation was ordered for Lake Charles and surrounding Calcasieu Parish.

That's when Dry Creek-sister picked up the phone and called Lake Charles-sister.

"Where are you going for the storm?"

Lake Charles-sister said, "I'm not sure."

"Well, I know where you're going. You're coming to stay with me in Dry Creek."

And that's precisely what happened.

The days and weeks after Rita were tough in Dry Creek. There was no water or electricity, and the storm's aftermath made every everyday tasks difficult, but according to the younger sister, it was a sweet time of forgiveness and healing.

They're both dead now, but I can attest to the fact that they stayed friends and caring sisters for the reminders of their lives.

I'm still touched by this story of forgiveness between those two Dry Creek sisters.

I hope it moved you, figuratively and literally. It moved and stirred your soul, but it also moved you to make the first step forward with your feet to heal any fall-outs in your life.

A Final Word

If you're in the midst of a falling-out, don't wait.

Last year, I sat by the deathbed of a dear friend who'd suffered a major stroke. I observed my precious aunt and uncle, who, although not related by blood, had been closer to my friend than family.

As their friend lay dying, I saw tears but no regret from my aunt and uncle. They'd been life-long friends, and nothing had been left unsaid.

Sadly, I observed blood family members, who had not spoken with their sister in twenty years, arrive.

They had lots of tears and a ton of regret. It's hard to restore a falling-out when one party is lying unconscious.

I'm sure there were two sides to this falling-out. It's nearly always that way.

My friend died estranged from her sisters. That's a burden they'll have to bear.

That makes it even sadder.

Don't wait.

Be the brave one and take the first step. Find some way of breaking the ice.

If you can't think of something to say, there's always chicken snakes and hurricanes.

Chapter 18

Know Those Who Serve

"Do unto others as you'd have them do unto you."

—Jesus in Luke 6:31

H is name was Raymond, and we were both about eighteen. It was unlikely we'd cross paths, much less become friends.

Raymond was a young black man from Pineville, and I was a country boy fresh from the Dry Creek woods.

He was the new janitor for our section of Tudor Hall, the men's dorm at Louisiana College.

I was brought up to be friendly, so I introduced myself to Raymond. I'd spent all of my teen summers working at church camp, doing custodial-style work. It taught me that all work has dignity when done well, and that served as common ground for our budding friendship.

Raymond and I became friends as we crossed paths daily. I think it happened because I learned his name.

Our casual friendship continued for my extended five-year college stay, even as Raymond moved up in his department. His success didn't surprise me. He was a conscientious worker who got along well with people.

* * *

Thirty years later, I returned to Louisiana College as a trustee. One day, while walking across campus, I saw Raymond. Like me, he'd aged, his hair and beard now peppered with gray, and I had my share of gray in the hair I had left. We greeted each other and laughed at how young we had been when we first met.

Raymond was now the college's maintenance director, which didn't surprise me. He was a man of character and class who did his job well.

During college, I made it my goal to learn the names of every custodian, cafeteria server, and maintenance worker on the campus. It's amazing how many friends you can make if you take the time to learn someone's name.

As I once read, "The greatest sound in the world is someone else saying your name."

A few years ago, I saw a hand-written sign in an African refugee camp:

"If you like people, people will like you."

It's true. When we take time to get to know people, good things happen.

It goes along with Jesus' most famous words, often known as the Golden Rule, *"Do unto others as you'd have them do unto you."*

When we acknowledge those who serve us we are helping fulfill that verse. Everyone wants to be noticed and appreciated.

Much of my work before and during college involved manual labor or menial service. It's amazing how people treat others as if they don't exist when they're doing "menial jobs."

I vowed then that I would ignore or be rude to anyone serving me and treat them with the dignity that any job done well deserves.

There's an interesting concept called "The Waiter Rule." Employers will take a prospective employee to a restaurant and carefully observe how this potential worker treats the wait staff. His can be the determining factor in the hire.

How we treat someone who serves us says a great deal about who we are.

* * *

During this season of my life, my primary job is pouring every drop of my life into the lives of my nine grandchildren. Please allow me the personal privilege of attaching a short note to them.

To: Noah, Jack, Jude, Luke, Sydney, Maggie, Emma, Ellen, and Eliza,

As you start a new school year, I want to challenge you to know the names of every service worker at your school. Greet them with the respect their service and age deserve.

Introduce yourself, learn their names and about their lives and families. Be a good listener. Everyone has amazing stories.

It's just good manners, and it goes hand-in-glove with Jesus' teaching of "Doing unto others . . ."

Know those who serve.

Chapter 19

The Red Cedars

M y 89-year-old mother proudly stands amidst a major landscaping of her front yard.

"You know it costs a lot."

I nod.

"You know I'm spending your inheritance."

I smile. My parents have already given me the best inheritance: a home filled with love, a good name, and a Godly example.

Mom walks to two small evergreen trees planted on each side of the sidewalk. They stand about head high.

"Momma, those trees are red cedars, just like the two giant cedars at the Old House."

She shakes her head. "I guess I won't see them grow that tall."

I won't either.

I look at her and the two saplings. I want to squeeze every drop of life with her.

The older I get, the more I realize that life is a giant rolling circle.

It's amazing if you stop long enough to look around.

The circle is rolling and spinning.

When the pecan tree fell across the roof of the Old House, the two giant cedars broke its fall, sparing the Old House more damage.

Several large cedar limbs were broken. We cut the limbs into small circular pieces for cup coasters. Every living member of the Frank and Dosia Iles clan received a coaster.

Red cedar is one of the prettiest woods. Its large heart is a beautiful rose color. Cedar is favored in construction for its beauty and rot-free nature.

My great-grandmother, Theodosia "Dosia" Wagnon Iles, recalled the two cedars as saplings during her childhood, thereby placing them older than 130 years.

Most pioneer homesteads had cedars in the front yard. Various stories abound: they brought good luck, and being evergreen reminded the settlers there was life beyond the grave.

I've always believed the early settlers simply enjoyed the cedar's beauty and shade. It probably reminded them of the front yards of their childhood homes back East.

Looking at our red cedars towering over the Old House front yard, I picture the two sisters, Dosia and Lou, frolicking in the yard, taking turns leaping over the young cedar saplings in front of their log cabin.

Theodosia was lovingly known as "Doten" to her family, who adored her deeply. Her parents, John Wesley Wagnon and Sarah Lyles Wagnon, traveled from Georgia as children with their families.

The Wagnons homesteaded along Dry Creek, while the Lyles settled further south on Barnes Creek.

When John Wagnon and Sarah Lyles fell in love and married, they homesteaded their own one hundred and twenty acres along a slow-moving stream called Crooked Bayou.

They built the simple log room that is the centerpiece of the Old House. Successive generations added rooms and porches to create what is now our unique family home.

Nearly every homeplace of that era featured a cedar in the yard.

The two cedars were planted by John and Sarah when they built their log cabin in about 1892.

The two cedars and the log room are still here.

John and Sarah Wagnon had two daughters, Louise and Theodosia.

Louise, "Aunt Lou," was a schoolteacher who never married. She lived her entire life on the Wagnon homestead. Although my generation never knew her, she is a rock-solid part of our heritage and should be remembered.

The second daughter, known as "Dosia," married Frank Iles, a member of another pioneer family. This was when the Iles name became associated with the Old House.

The importance and impact of the two Wagnon sisters, Lou and Dosia, and Dosia's husband, Frank Iles,

"Pa" and "Doten," as Frank and Dosia were known by family, had one son, Lloyd Iles, my grandfather.

"PaPa Lloyd" married Pearl Stockwell ("MaMa Pearl"), and they had six Iles children. These generations had dual citizenship between Dry Creek and De-Ridder. During the work week, they lived in DeRidder, while weekends and summers were spent in Dry Creek.

Lloyd and Pearl's children, Clayton, Lloydell, Margie Nell, Bill, JoAnn, and Clint, grew up in a rich environment surrounded by three generations of Iles and Wagnons.

Eight heirs currently own the Old House and its acreage: Bill Iles, JoAnn Iles Edwards, Curt Iles, Colleen Iles Glaser, Claudia Iles Campbell, Jeff Mullican, Jess Mullican, and Jo Sarah Mullican Harrell.

Our generation will eventually pass on this legacy to descendants of the next generation of the Wagnon/Iles clan.

They'll inherit the Old House, the two red cedars, and our land along Crooked Bayou Swamp. I'm confident they'll be good stewards, and I'm pretty sure the two red cedars will still be here.

Chapter 20

Lloyd's Teeth

Lloyd and Lana have always been one of my favorite couples. I'd describe Lloyd as *dapper,* friendly, and impressive. His wife Lana is vivacious, looking twenty years younger than her age and possessing a contagious laugh.

Lana told the following story from the early years of their marriage.

She and Lloyd were on a Florida beach vacation. While enjoying the surf, a rogue wave knocked them down, and Lloyd lost his false teeth.

They searched the beach daily to no avail.

For the rest of the vacation, Lana ate fresh Gulf seafood, while Lloyd's eating options were very limited.

Before leaving for home, Lana left their mailing address at the beachfront hotel, and the management promised to mail the teeth should they show up.

Lloyd and Lana had never expected to hear from the hotel, so they were pleasantly surprised when a package containing Lloyd's false teeth arrived.

He put the teeth in. They didn't fit.

Lana said, "I wonder who else is looking for their teeth? Because we've got their pair."

Lana told this story with cackling laughter. Lloyd, a good sport, grinned sheepishly with his new teeth.

It has always been one of my favorite stories.

When Lloyd died, Lana asked me to give a eulogy. I was so honored, and I asked Lana, "Should I tell Lloyd's false teeth story?"

She smiled, "Curt, of course. It would only be *fitting* for you to share."

I warned the attendees. "I have Lana's permission to tell this story, and you have her permission to laugh out loud."

And they did.

* * *

There was so much more to my friend Lloyd Weldon than his false teeth. He was a man of character, a hard worker who provided for his family, and a Godly man. Lloyd was a dedicated and wonderful husband and father.

I'm so glad he was my friend.

Chapter 21

Will You Forgive Me?

Here's a good quote:

"An unforgiving Christian? That's an oxymoron."

-Jordy McCaskill

My friend and I had just finished a fine meal at Word-of-Mouth Cafe near the Rapides Parish Courthouse in downtown Alexandria.

As we neared my truck, a tall security guard got in my face and scolded me. "You cannot park here. This is only for the courthouse, and I saw where you came from."

The guard ambushed me and really got in my grill. He was much taller and younger and seemed to enjoy showing who was the boss and putting me in my place.

He had me back on my heels. I glanced at my friend, who stood speechless.

I caught my breath. I was ready to go toe to toe with the security guard. He reminded me of the proverbial "Big Man" in Africa, who enjoyed flexing his power and authority.

Suddenly, I recalled something I'd learned ten years ago in Africa. I turned to the security guard. "I am so sorry. Will you please forgive me?"

"What?"

"Mister, I'm sorry that I parked in the wrong spot." I caught his eyes. "I'm sorry. Will you please forgive me?"

He took a step back and started sputtering. He was clearly exasperated.

Suddenly, he was *back on his heels.*

With one simple sentence, I had wrested control of the entire encounter away from the guard.

He was no longer in charge. I was.

Here's another thing about my "apology." It took the big man off guard.

Finally, he resignedly waved me away, "OK, just don't do it again."

As we got in the truck, my friend asked, "What was that all about?"

I laughed. "Three years in Africa taught me a lot."

When I first arrived in Africa in 2013, I was terrified whenever a policeman waved me to the side of the road. This was especially true in the wild west country of South Sudan and Upcountry Uganda.

When the police saw my Toyota Land Cruiser approaching, they licked their chops.

I called it "DWW. Driving While White."

The reasons for being stopped were endless, "I have stopped you. You have mud on your headlights,"

Or "Mzee, I am sorry, but your fire extinguisher tag has expired. I must give you a ticket."

My personal favorite was, "No. No. No. You are carrying luggage in the back seat. That is illegal. You can only carry passengers on the seats."

Another jewel was the policeman handing the ticket book to you through the window. "Here. You must find *yourself.*"

All of these infractions had one common denominator: the policeman wanted a bribe.

These encounters often occurred at a barricade operated by a handful of guards or soldiers.

I rolled down my window as the policeman cited a litany of misdemeanors and felonies I'd committed against the government of South Sudan.

Then the officer stood upright, slowly shaking his head, "I must take you to the station."

Up to this point, he'd been subtle about asking, *"Do you have something for the gate?" or "Do you have some tea money?"*

I was ready. "The company I work for forbids giving bribes. If I do that, I could lose my job. You don't want that, do you?"

A look of hurt would flash across his face. "Oh, no. I would never ask for a bribe, but I still must take you to the station."

The "no-bribe missionary company" answer usually worked, but it wouldn't deter the real professionals. They'd stand at the car window with an open palm and say, "Tea money, or I still must take you to the station."

When nothing else worked, it was time to unleash my secret weapon.

I learned to disarm a bribe shakedown with, **"I am sorry. Will you please forgive me?"**

It was the magical eight words. In African culture, you cannot ignore an apology, especially from a Mzee (elder) with gray in his beard.

I observed many reactions to the *magical eight words*: shock, resignation, humor, and sighs in multiple languages.

As needed, I'd add, "As your *Mzee* (Father), I'm asking you to forgive me."

Africans have great respect for their elders. The forgiveness card and the gray-bearded elder usually worked.

The result was always the same. The policeman would wave us on after making me promise not to repeat this serious offense.

I want to be honest. I have a Southern rebel bloodline in me and those eight magical words don't come easy, especially when I hadn't done a dadgum thing wrong and was still being shaken down.

I want to return to those two sentences:

"I am sorry. Will you please forgive me?"

It's pride that keeps us from saying the words. Don't let pride rob you of the joy of a possible reconciliation.

Even if it doesn't go well, you've done your part.

It didn't hurt me to say the eight words on a dirt road in rural Africa.

I have to admit it's much more difficult in our American culture. We're a prideful people.

I bet someone in your orbit needs to hear it from you.

I'd advise you to stand in front of a mirror and practice the eight magical words before apologizing.

The words come much easier when you've practiced them.

*However, a word of caution is in order. Avoid the deadly ninth word,

But.

"But" has ruined many perfectly good apologies.

"But ... you,"

I don't know if you've heard the term "TOB." That's Transfer of Blame.

TOB *Transfer of Blame.*

It has no place in any sincere apology.

L.S.U. baseball hero Warren Morris said it was Coach Skip Bertman's favorite acronym, TOB—transfer of blame.

TOB.

It'd be a good tattoo for your right forearm. No TOB!

"I'm sorry. Please forgive me, *but ...*

Transfer of blame often has the dangerous *but* lurking in the apology.

That's when the apology explodes.

"But you made me do it ... " No one can make you do anything. Look in the mirror!

I've waited for all of this chapter to say this. "Get your buts out of here!

Don't do it, man. Put a question mark at the end of your apology, not a comma.

TOB. It's human nature to want to blame someone else. It goes back to the Garden, but that doesn't make it right.

No "But." "No TOB."

Do this: "I am so sorry. Will you please forgive me?"

* * *

Remember I.A.S.W.Y.P.F.M. as in "I am sorry. Will you please forgive me? "

Resist the urge to put a but-comma after "Please forgive me."

That's how those pesky buts sneak in.

No buts. No TOB. Stop it!

A final word on African bribes

Knowing we'd be stopped when we traveled up-country, DeDe devised a novel plan. We carried three things in our vehicle: bottles of water, Bibles in several dialects, and fresh banana bread.

It's another part of African culture. You cannot refuse a gift.

A loaf of DeDe's homemade banana bread always did the trick. We enjoyed the surprised look of a policeman holding a loaf of fresh banana bread in his outstretched hand. It wasn't the kind of bread he wanted, but his culture forced him to accept it with good grace.

With a smile of resignation, he motioned me forward with his free hand, "Open the gate and let Mzee through."

He had his bribe, and we were on my way north. I thanked him as we sped by.

I glanced in the rearview mirror. Five policemen were standing at the gate, hands on their hips. One of them had a loaf of banana bread in his right hand.

As they say in Swahili, Kwaheri.

That's Goodbye.

"Am I the kind of man

That you think is strong,

But stand up in a crowd

And say, *I was wrong.*"

—"Am I the Kind of Man"

Toy Caldwell/Marshall Tucker Band

Chapter 22

The Hobyahs

"And I can still hear my old hound dog barkin'
Chasin' down a hoodoo there
Chasin' down a hoodoo there
Born the Bayou
Born on the Bayou."

—John Fogerty

"Born on the Bayou"

I t's a scary night when the Hobyahs slither out of Crooked Bayou Swamp.

My forebearers didn't fear goblins or werewolves. Our ancestral family had its own *haints*. They were called "Hobyahs," slimy creatures that slithered out of Crooked Bayou Swamp at night.

Every ancient rural culture has had a host of fairy-tale-like stories about buga-boos, werewolves, monsters, and bogie men—stories told to scare the bejabbers out of children.

These stories were often told for protection to keep a child from wandering off in the dark night where a host of catty-wampuses, flesh-eating wolves, banshees, and dark, sleek panthers waiting to gobble you up.

It's called the "Folklore of Fear" and is found in every civilization. Folklorists call them "Beast Tales," which nearly always occurred at night.

Remarkably, kids are still drawn to these gothic stories of the unknown. They love being thrilled and terrified at the same time.

When I read *The Hobbit* to my three boys at bedtime, I usually mimicked Gollum's slimy voice: *"My precious."* Our son Clint would pull the covers over his head, but the next night he was back for more.

The Lord of the Rings is a beast story. You've got Gollum, wargs, orcs, and evil sorcerers. It's enough to make any small hobbit or seven-year-old run for cover.

* * *

The story of the Hobyahs originated as a Scottish folk tale that was passed down orally through generations.

Eventually, the Hobyahs booked passage on ships to Australia and America.

The Australians used the fear of the Hobyahs to scare their children into not wandering off into the bush, where dingoes and other wild things were waiting to eat them.

The Hobyahs were also carried into America by the hardy Scot-Irish pioneers who took root in the Appalachians.

When the American mountain clans migrated south and west, they brought the Hobyahs with them until the story ended up on the porch of the Old House in Dry Creek.

My Dad's sister, Aunt Lloydell Iles Mullican, inscribed the following in the flyleaf of my personal copy of *The Hobyahs*. Here are her words:

"My Great Aunt, Louise Wagnon, or as we called her 'Aunt Lou,' was the appointed nightly storyteller. During the hot summer nights, we would sleep on mattresses or pallets in the hallway of the Old House, and Aunt Lou would lower her voice and tell bedtime stories.

"One of my favorites was about the Hobyahs. If you closed your eyes as Aunt Lou told the story, you could see, feel, and hear the strange creatures called Hobyahs.

"She'd lower her voice, 'They came creep, creep, creeping on their thorny toes and on their scaly knees, come the slimy, slippery Hobyahs.'

"We knew for sure that the Hobyahs had once lived deep in the darkness of Crooked Bayou Swamp behind the Old House. Maybe they still did.

"The hero of the story was Little Dog Turpie, whose incessant barking kept the home safe from the nightly visitors.

"Aunt Lou would startle us. *'Out jumped Little Dog Turpie*. He chased the Hobyahs through the deep, dark, damp swamp. He chased them over the mountains and far away, and the Hobyahs never returned.'

"I felt safe knowing Little Dog Turpie had chased them away forever. I also felt secure knowing Aunt Lou was nearby. She made us all feel safe.

"Even though we were terrified, we begged to hear the Hobyah story the next night."

* * *

I think about my ancestors— my uncles and aunts— hearing those stories in the light of the fireplace or the coal oil lamp on the porch.

I can imagine them squeezing together in a protective ball as they listen for the distant howl of the Hobyahs or Little Turpie's comforting bark.

* * *

Aunt Lloydell closed her inscription in my copy of *The Hobyahs* in her unique handwriting:

"Curt, I hope you will share this story with your children and grandchildren.

Love,

Aunt Lloydell Iles Mullican."

Aunt Loydell, I've passed the Hobyahs to my clan. Now, I'm taking the next step in passing this story on to my readers. They'll hear Aunt Lou's story, add to it, make it their own, and tell it to generations to come.

I believe Aunt Lou would be pleased with that—Aunt Lloydell, I think you would be, too.

* * *

Readers, I have one request. When you tell your version of the Hobyahs to your children, and they ask where the story came from, say that it came from Aunt Lou, who lived in the Old House on the edge of Crooked Bayou Swamp.

* * *

Mary Louise Wagnon was born in 1891. She lived her entire life in Dry Creek at the Old House, built by her parents, John and Sarah Lyles Wagnon.

Aunt Lou was an elementary school teacher who never married and was the most beloved member of my generation of the Iles/Wagnon clan. Louise Wagnon died in 1954, two years before I was born. She is buried beside her parents in Lyles Cemetery near Reeves, Louisiana.

One of the longings of my heart is that I never knew her.

Then, maybe I did.

Lloydell Iles Mullican was my Dad's younger sister. She was the primary bridge between our ancestors and my generation. Aunt Lloydell loved the old stories and was the caretaker of our family letters and photos, which date back to the mid-nineteenth century. She passed those treasures on to her granddaughter Jessica Mullican and her younger sister JoAnn Iles Edwards.

Appropriately, Aunt Lloydell is buried next to her beloved Aunt Lou in Lyles Cemetery.

* * *

It's on my future Creekbank books bucket list: an updated children's picture book entitled *The Hobyahs of Crooked Bayou Swamp.*

I'm sure Aunt Lou and Aunt Lloydell will be making cameo appearances.

It should be fun.

Chapter 23

Leaving the World a Better Place

"He went through life oiling squeaky doors."

Leave this world better than you found it!

"L.T.W.B.T.Y.F.I."

I read about a man who spent his life oiling squeaky doors. He carried a small can of three-in-one oil and was always looking for offenders,

It's amazing what a few drops of oil will do on the hinges of a door.

He went through life oiling doors. Evidently it was his calling, and he performed with dedication.

Someone might say that's such a minor act. Well, they've never had the hair-on-the-back-of-their-neck stand at the nerve-shattering sound of a rusty hinge.

Maybe I exaggerate, but you get the picture.

It should be in the back pocket of every living, breathing human being: do something to make a difference.

Plant a tree you'll never sit under. It's a selfless act.

The best time to plant a tree is twenty years ago. The second-best time is today.

So, get out there and plant.

Whatever we touch. Wherever we go. We ought to leave it better.

Mother Teresa said it well, "Not all of us can do great things, but we can do small things with great love."

* * *

I recall "Pop" Schales. I never knew his given name, and we never spoke, but in my child's mind, he had the best job in Ward 7 or 8:

Pop Schales directed traffic onto Highway 113 after each East Beauregard Trojan home basketball game. He had a flashlight with a red extension and he stood waving at the main entrance to the parking lot. I can't remember him wearing a badge or uniform, but he had a job and it was safely directing traffic onto the highway after ballgames.

That red flashlight caught my attention. To my child-like mind, it seemed magical and I secretly coveted one like it.

Our school, East Beauregard High School, had three entrance gates, each with a cattleguards.

Don't laugh. I bet few of you can boast of having three cattle gaps at your school. This was a necessary need due to the open range and wandering cattle.

Pop Schales would take his spot at the main entrance cattleguard flagging traffic to ensure good flow from all three gates as they merged onto 113.

Some of you are laughing at the idea of a traffic jam on Louisiana Highway 113, but that means you never attended an East Beauregard basketball game during the 1960s. The Trojans had an excellent team featuring hard-nosed defense and an up-tempo style. Folks came from all over Beauregard Parish to pack the gym.

After the game, Pop Schales would be out there, red flashlight waving, directing three lines of traffic merging onto the main highway.

As we drove past him, my young mind thought. *I'd sure like to have a red flashlight like that.*

It was years later that I realized he was doing what some might call a small job, but he did it with commitment. I also doubt if he was assigned the job as traffic director. He probably just showed up with his red flashlight and went to work.

And showing up is a big part of any job.

That's why, a half-century after his death, I still remember him waving that long red flashlight. That's why he's come alive again on the pages of this book.

Small things with great love.

Get out there with passion and get something done.

Bishop Jake Owenby calls it "Living a full-throated life."

I like the sound of that.

The full-throated life.

Don't just stand there—live life to the hilt. Be full-throated.

* * *

I've always loved camping and hiking. Part of the joy is setting up camp along a bubbling mountainside creek or under tall forested pines. After breaking camp, I carefully clean the place. I like the thought that no one will even know a human has stayed here.

Many times, at popular campsites, you'll find trash in the fire pit or other signs of thoughtless humans who've passed. Often I'll load up their trash and carry it out.

That's what difference-makers do.

Some folks toss out trash.

Others pick it up.

It's your call.

My pastor, David Brooks, has a well-known habit: He rescues shopping carts—not just his empty cart but any strays in the vicinity—and places them in the receptacle area.

Leaving this world a better place.

It's just a matter of respect.

It is a matter of stewardship. Leaving this world better than we got it.

Make a difference in your own way in your world.

Put a dent in the universe. It doesn't have to be big to be great.

"If you cannot feed a hundred people, feed one."

One of my favorite comedians, Jim Carrey, said it well,

"The effect you have on others is the most valuable currency you have."

* * *

Recently, I came across another great quote:

"See Dirt? Throw Seeds!"

That perfectly describes what we should be doing.

Where and *how* you throw your seeds is a very personal decision. It's your personal decision.

However, I urge you to make it.

Leave this world better than you found it.

Everyone has a purpose to fulfill.

John Maxwell says, "Find your *why,* and you'll find your *way*."

L.T.W.B.T.Y.F.I!

Chapter 24

Blackjack Oaks and Porch Lizards

"Mary, there are two things I'm asking you not to do. Don't cut those two blackjacks behind your new house, and don't let anyone kill the lizards at the Old House. They're each a special part of our heritage."

—My great-grandmother's words to my mother when we moved to Dry Creek in 1960.

I f you took a poll of most American foresters, they'd agree that the lowly blackjack oak is the homeliest and ugliest of all our native trees. It's no accident that they're called scrub oaks in the Deep South,

They're the ugly step-sisters of our tall, majestic longleafs.

The soil of the Pineywoods is sandy and loamy. It's the perfect soil for the native longleafs and blackjacks. It's the same soil that grows the best watermelons in America.

* * *

As I've shared earlier, my great-grandmother Theodosia Wagnon was known in Dry Creek as Dosia. Her first grandchildren twisted it to Doten.

*Dot*en. That became her name for every succeeding generation.

She explained to my mom, "Mary, the blackjack is the natural tree of our Piney-woods along with the longleafs. You'll find blackjack oaks growing around the fringe of any field of pines."

In 2012, I cleared my land and planted twelve acres of longleaf pines by hand. I left a row of blackjacks along the south property line.

One of the joys of my life has been watching my longleafs grow, but I also walk to the south property line and pay my respects to the row of scraggly, unsightly blackjacks.

When we moved into our new house in 1960, there were two scraggly blackjacks in the backyard.

They were ugly at first, but over the years, they became special. They became landmarks in my parents' backyard.

Those two-lifetime blackjacks died during the 2023 drought. They're dropping limbs and leaning towards Mom's back porch.

Doten didn't say anything about cutting dead blackjacks, so I think it's fine.

I'm going to miss them. They are one of the many connections to my ancestors.

* * *

Lizards—they are easy to catch, but they are found even in kings' palaces.

-Proverbs 30:28

Doten's other request to Mom was to leave the lizards alone: "Mary, please leave those porch lizards alone at the Old House."

When we lived at the Old House, they weren't just *porch* lizards. They were *house* lizards.

Because of the draftiness of the house, lizards lurked in every room. You got used to them. There wasn't much choice.

Doten would say, "Baby, don't hurt those lizards. They're as much a part of the old place as we are."

So, for me, they are one of the things that make the Old House so special.

I've been told that I'm sentimental beyond sensibility.

Yes, I am, and that's why I love porch lizards.

A male is showing his money on the porch railing. He's surveying his kingdom like Leonardo DiCaprio on the bow of the *Titanic*, "I'm the King of the World.!"

Mister Lizard puffs his red sac, advertising on his own personal billboard, "I'm the *real* King of the World."

Then, he adds, "And I'm looking for a woman to call my own, and I'm available for love."

He's right. In this small section of the railing over to the screen door, he is king of the lizard world at least in his small reptilian mind.

He'll get no argument from me in the red rocker. I enjoy his show: running ten paces, puffing up his neck, still looking for that elusive girlfriend.

* * *

Many people are fearful of lizards and would never touch one. I respect their fear. We all have some phobia. My personal demon is a fear of heights, but I've never feared lizards; I've caught them since I was a child.

I still do.

My favorite parlor tricks were lizard-earrings, belly-rubbing hypnosis, and holding a green lizard against the brown bark of a tree. Watching it quickly camouflage its colors is one of the wonders of the modern world, at least in my book.

I've never ceased to be amazed at his ability to adapt to his environment. This won't be the last time I share my credo:

Stay Curious.

Be Amazed.

Share Stories.

I'm equally astonished when I toss the lizard into the tall grass, and he soon becomes "Invisible."

The only times I've mistreated a lizard were to catch one and show off parlor tricks to my grandchildren.

I'm sure if I harmed one, Doten would rise up out of her grave and thump me on the back of the head.

Baby, don't hurt a lizard. They're our friends.

I've never forgotten that.

It's winter as I write this. The Old House lizards are holed up wherever reptiles go in the cold.

I'll know it's spring when I see a lizard run along the porch railing.

Go ahead, fellow. Show us what you got.

The green anole lizard can live up to eight years in the wild. I'd surmise that very few survive to that age.

The one I'm watching today is a direct descendant of the lizards Doten observed as a child.

It's been one hundred and thirty years since she was a child.

132 years. The average lizard's lifespan is eight years. You do the math.

I'm the fifth generation of my family to sit on this porch. Mr. Lizard can brag about many, many more generations of ancestors who've lived on this porch.

Yesterday, I was at the Old House. As the kitchen screen door slammed, a brown lizard scurried under the table.

I kneel. "Hey, Buddy. Don't run off too quickly. You and I are kin. Our families have shared this house for generations."

He ignores me as he escapes through a crack in the floor.

A lot of things have changed, but the lizards are still here.

May they always be.

As I mentioned above, I've never hurt or killed a lizard.

I was raised better than that.

I've also never cut down a blackjack oak.

If I did either, I fear that my great-grandmother would come out of her grave and chastise me. But that's not my greatest fear. It's that I'd disappoint her.

Yes, she's been dead for sixty years but still casts a revered shadow across our Iles clan.

To me, Doten was the connection between the old pioneer Dry Creek and the small community where I came to age in the mid-twentieth century.

She was also the glue that held our family together through tragedy, trials, and life.

Doten wasn't perfect. She dipped Garrett Sweet Snuff, among other vices. It was nasty and seemed out of character. I seemed prone to knocking over her spit cup, which she tried to hide beneath the couch leg.

You don't want to see a tipped snuff spit can on a rug. It ain't a pretty sight.

Her name was Nancy Theodosia Wagnon.

That's a memorable name: Theodosia.

You probably won't find it in any baby name books.

I believed she'd made a great character on "Downtown Abbey." Mr. Carson speaks precisely, "May I present Grand Dame Nancy Theodisa Wagnon-Iles."

She was known as Dosia among her family and in Dry Creek.

Her first grandchildren had trouble pronouncing "Dosia," so she became "Doten."

That's what we still call her when we talk about her. Less than ten of her descendants left knew her.

She married Frank Iles from the "Who'd a Thought It School" community.

They were my paternal great-grandparents. No matter what I write, I seem to return to sitting at their feet.

After a lifetime of writing, journaling, and publishing, I seem to return to this porch continually.

The log and kitchen part of the house was built around 1890.

Doten left a lasting legacy about things like blackjack oaks and porch lizards, but her most enduring lesson shaped my life-view.

I shared earlier how she passed on her love of the Pineywoods, but there's another lesson she taught me,

She showed me how to die.

In addition to the love of nature Doten passed on, she willed something more memorable.

She was the spiritual mother of our family.

Even for a generation like me who didn't know her long enough.

Even those future generations who'll not remember her name. The spiritual thread that runs through our family came from her faith and life.

Two occurrences from Doten's deathbed shaped my worldview of death and the afterlife. I wasn't there in the hospital room, but my daddy related that day to me.

Doten was a worrier. If there weren't something available to worry about, she'd create one out of whole cloth.

Her name was Theodosia Wagnon Iles, but we called her "Doten."

Theodosia. I'm disappointed, but not surprised, that no one named a daughter after her.

She was my paternal great-grandmother.

In Dry Creek, she was known as Dosia, but her grandchildren called her Doten. That's how I remember her Doten.

That's why Doten's dying words still resonate in my soul.

Doten had a life-long fear of death. All of my older relatives spoke of it. They said she lived with a great dread of dying throughout her eighty-plus years.

* * *

Cancer runs in my family. Doten, dying of cancer, was placed in the Beauregard Baptist Hospital in DeRidder. My father, who was there on her dying day, shared two statements about her dying moment.

"All of my life, I've dreaded this moment. And now that it's here, it's not that bad at all," she said.

A few minutes later, she tried to rise up in the bed, lifted her arms, and said, "I see Jesus, and I can nearly touch him."

Within minutes, she was dead.

Her two deathbed statements stuck in my seven-year-old mind.

Half a century later, they're still there.

Doten lived her life in fear of something we all must face—but something we need not fear when we are prepared.

When that time came, she did not face it alone but with Jesus.

Others may surmise she had a hallucination, but I simply believe she realized she was stepping over into another life.

If my great-grandmother said she saw Jesus coming to get her, then I'll take her (and His) word about it.

I've chosen to believe every word of the Bible about life after death.

Additionally, I have the deathbed testimony of my great-grandmother. I believe it, too. If Doten said it, I believe it. She was our rock.

I've built my life on the words of the one she trusted: Jesus.

Each time death has brushed up against my life, I hear His words at the grave of Lazarus:

I am the resurrection and the life. He who believes in me will live, even though he dies, and whoever lives and believes in me will never die."

—John 11:25-26

Doten, thanks for cementing my view of death and everlasting life in Jesus. You lived much of your life in fear of death, but thanks to your final earthly words, I've never feared death or lizards.

Your best lessons were about the woods, legacy, and a deep love for family.

But your most enduring lesson about life came from your last words spoken at death.

Thank you, Doten.

A prayer about legacy:

Lord, I thank you for my roots.

Lord, I want to leave those same enduring footprints on the life road of my children, grandchildren, and even great-grandchildren.

Help me, Lord.

May my words be few but wise.

May I seize each opportunity to set an example

Of the things that *really* matter.

And, as always, remind me

That those things that matter aren't really things.

They're lessons.

They're words.

They're stories.

They're people.

It always comes down to people.

Thanks for calling me to be a storyteller and allowing me to tell these stories of *my people.*

Please help me not to miss the stories and lessons I yet have to learn.

Amen.

P.S. And Lord, I thank you for blackjack oaks and porch lizards. Amen and Amen.

Chapter 25

The Unoffended Life

"Don't throw your sucker on the ground

unless you're willing to eat a dirty sucker."

—Dewitt Daigre

Unrestrained anger can be destructive in the life of any man or woman,

They do and say things in the heat of battle.

If you're angry all of the time, you'd better be ready to eat lots of dirty suckers.

The answer to this is the unoffended life. It's the best way to live.

What is the unoffendable life?

It's the mark of a person who doesn't easily get bent out of shape. They don't carry a chip on their shoulder. They let offenses roll off their back and choose to overlook slights, real or perceived.

In this chapter, I'll use the masculine pronoun "he" for clarity, but this asset applies equally to men and women.

The unoffended person chooses not to hold grudges. He understands that there is no heavier load to carry than a grudge.

He believes, "If you like people, people will like you." He realizes that relationships always trump harsh words.

The unoffended man is good-natured. He's chosen to develop the habit of being cheerful.

Webster describes *good-naturedness* as "having a pleasant disposition and displaying an easygoing manner, especially in social situations."

The unoffended man oozes *graciousness.*

Listen to Paul's words in Colossians 4:6: *Let your speech always be gracious, seasoned with salt, so that you may know how you ought to answer each person.*

You ask, "What is the definition of graciousness?"

I'm unsure, but you'll know when you see it.

It seems that the most challenging fight we have to live unoffended is in traffic. Driving a car brings out the worst in people, and we must choose how to respond.

Deciding to stay calm, not get rattled, ignore gestures and curse words, and smile at aggressive men in huge F-150 Ford trucks.

I always think when I'm cut off or gestured at by some fist-shaking angry man, *Some poor woman's got to live with that jerk.*

God love her.

I say the same thing about an aggressive woman driver, but I use a slightly descriptive *word.*

You can take it from there.

I've made up my mind to be a calm driver.

I seldom honk unless there's a stray dog in the road.

It's hard to honk politely unless you're honking the "shave-and-a hair-cut-two-bits honk. It takes good manual dexterity and finger motor control, but it'll never be returned with a middle finger.

If you're not familiar with that friendly honk, go to YouTube.

Looking back, I can't recall my Daddy firing a shot or a honk in anger.

My father, Clayton Iles, who lived from 1934 to 2003, was a gracious and unoffended man.

I keep returning to my Dad because he was so remarkable. He still lives through my writing and four generations of Ilese.

He had all the traits of an unoffended man: self-effacing, humorous, forgiving, and unfailing in his belief in seeing the best in others.

Above all, Daddy was comfortable in his own skin wherever he went.

He would've been as relaxed and winsome in the Oval Office as he was at the Dry Creek Community Catfish Lunch. In either venue, if asked, he would've burst out in his favorite song (and mine as well), "The Wayfaring Stranger:"

"I am just going over Jordan.

I am just going over home."

Let me be clear: Clayton Iles wasn't perfect, but he was consistent. My father at home was no different than the public man.

I can honestly say that when Daddy died, he did not have one single enemy.

That says a lot.

The unoffended man doesn't fly off the handle.

To become an unoffended person takes practice. It's a habit like any other.

I'm still working on it. I have a ways to go. One way I'm learning to be unoffended is the part of writing I detest.

Rejection letters.

It's part of the life of a professional writer.

Rejection letters. You'll have a stack of them if you're sending out book proposals.

I've learned not to take it personally.

To accept it with graciousness.

I send a courteous note to the editor, trying to glean anything from their rejection. That painful letter only spurs my determination to be published.

I take that rejection and channel it into an inner fire to write and prove them wrong,

The book you're holding is a product of that grit and perseverance.

Learn from everyone, always remembering,

You have no friends; you have no enemies; you only have teachers.

Additionally, I'm learning to accept life's setbacks and difficulties with a smile, "Oh, don't worry about that. I'll just put it in the next book."

How you look at something goes a long way toward being unflappable and unoffendable.

The confident, unoffended man doesn't have to get in the last word. Sometimes, he chooses to bite off his tongue. He knows that sometimes, the best answer to ignorance is silence.

Because silence can speak volumes.

Living an unoffended life is not a sign of weakness. It doesn't entail being run over, pushed around, or exploited. It is a sign of inner strength and peace.

The unoffended man knows there are hills to die on.

There's a time and place to dig in and take a stand, but the unoffended man understands these skirmishes are few and far between, so he chooses his battles carefully.

There's no chip on his shoulder.

He attempts to cut people slack, remembering that folks often act a certain way because they have a rock in their shoe.

He chooses his reactions to people and events. When confronted with road rage, he'll give a sad shrug followed by, "I bet he's hell to live with,"

Or an equally strong, "I'd hate to be married to her."

Richard Carlson's excellent book *Don't Sweat the Small Stuff* speaks of this concept of being unoffendable.

Please take note of the subtitle: *And It's All Small Stuff).*

The unoffendable person overlooks the minor irritations of life. As Solomon, the wisest man of the Bible, wrote

"He that is slow to anger is better than the mighty, and he that ruleth his spirit than he that taketh a city."

—Proverbs 16:32

General George C. Marshall was a leading figure of the 20th Century. He oversaw the American war effort, coordinating the two-front war that led to the defeat of Nazi Germany and Imperial Japan.

After the War, Marshall served as Secretary of State and designed the Marshall Plan, which helped post-war Western Europe recover from the perils of Communism.

He was famous for his sense of integrity and commitment to the job at hand.

The following excerpt is from *George C. Marshall: Defender of the Republic* by David L. Roll. It concerns President Roosevelt's decision to keep Marshall in Washington and assign the D-Day invasion, Operation Overlord, to Dwight Eisenhower.

"Marshall said it was presumptuous for him to suggest that his role as chief of staff was more important than a field command. This was the code he lived by. At that moment, the quintessential moment after the president asked him what he wanted to do, Marshall was utterly selfless.

"It was Henry Stimson, Secretary of War and a lifelong Presbyterian, who found an apt proverb. 'He that ruleth his spirit is better than he that taketh a city.'"

I close with several lines from my favorite Jerry Jeff Walker song "The Stranger"

"He was the kind who'd pay no mind

When he was bumped into.

He was the kind that let you find out

All that he knew.

He never got uptight, never started a fight,

Never threw so much as a dart.

He was a man after my own heart.

And I loved him.

I loved him true."

(Lyrics by Jerry Merrick)

Chapter 26

Think Before You Shoot

"If I had a time machine,□
I'd go back to when panthers roamed in Arkansas,

And buffalo made their home in Tennessee."

-Kate Campbell

"When Panthers Roamed in Arkansas"

I t wasn't a panther, and it sure wasn't a buffalo.

It was an American Lynx: *Lynx canadensis.*

A lynx is "a wild cat with yellowish-brown fur (sometimes spotted), a short tail, and tufted ears, found chiefly in the northern latitudes of North America and Eurasia."

Jerry Clower called it "a souped-up wildcat."

An encounter with a lynx can be dangerous.

In more ways than one.

* * *

Some things cannot be taken back.

That's a good reason to choose carefully what you do and say.

Rule 1: Think first, then shoot.

Rule 2: If in doubt, don't shoot.

The best example is when you pull the trigger of a gun.

Once that bullet or shell leaves the barrel, there's no taking it back.

I have a Pineywoods friend who learned this lesson the hard way on a Colorado elk hunt.

On the day of this story, he had no luck with bagging an elk, but while on his stand, a lynx strode out of the rocks.

We don't have lynxes in Louisiana, only its smaller cousin, the bobcat.

In Pineywoods, Louisiana, any predator is known by the colloquial term "varmints."

I'd define a varmint as any animal that can damage your crops or livestock.

This list would include raccoons, foxes, feral hogs, crows, coyotes . . . and bobcats.

* * *

My friend carefully put his scope on the Colorado lynx. I would say that's the default reaction of most men I've grown up with. We always shoot a varmint. He took a deep breath and pulled the trigger.

Click.

His hunting rifle misfired. He later told me, "It was God telling me not to shoot."

He ejected the shell, reloaded, and fired.

There was one less Colorado lynx in the Rocky Mountains.

Proud of his unique kill, my friend brought the dead lynx back to the hunting camp.

Everyone gathered around in admiration at the large lynx, and other interested parties soon joined them.

Several four-wheelers, manned by Federal game agents, roared into camp. They were soon joined by a helicopter that landed in a nearby flat spot.

A stern agent walked to the hunters. "Where's the lynx and the man who shot it?"

My friend, an honest man, stepped forward. "I'm the one."

He had no idea what trouble he was in. Lynxes are a federally protected species in Colorado, and this one had a radio collar.

They quickly arrested my friend, confiscated his rifle and four-wheeler, and hauled him to jail.

He had to post a high bail to get out and return to Beauregard Parish. He left behind his gun, 4-wheeler, and gear and faced an upcoming court date.

The case made national news due to the role of the lynx population in an ongoing battle between Colorado developers and environmentalists. As long as the lynx is federally protected, new subdivisions and mountain resorts cannot be built in its domain.

My friend, shaking his voice, told me, "They're going to make an example of me. I could get up to a year in jail and a stiff fine."

"When my gun misfired the first time, I should've taken it as a sign from God not to shoot that lynx. I was just too stubborn and fired up not to shoot the second time." He shook his head. "Once you pull that trigger, you can't take it back."

It got me thinking about how many things in life are irrevocable.

I've pulled the trigger.

Harsh words to a loved one or stranger.

A shove or fist thrust in anger.

I have another friend, Paul, who is an avid deer hunter. When I see him at the mill, he re-lives his latest hunts. Recently, he said something that really stuck with me: "Don't pull that trigger until you are absolutely sure."

How many tragedies could've been avoided by following Paul's simple adage?

It's especially true with our words.

That childhood saying, "Sticks and stones may break my bones, but words will never hurt me," is a crock of bull corn.

Words can wound or affirm.

And every one of us can painfully recall something said to us that still cuts like a knife when recalled.

Sadly, we all know how many times we've said something, usually in a moment of heat, to a family member.

Just like the lynxes' fatal bullet, what we say cannot be taken back.

That's why we should choose our words carefully and, when needed, walk wordlessly away until our temper cools and we can speak with some perspective and a sense of respect.

It's especially the key to a good marriage. I'm amazed at how spouses often harshly speak to each other but would never talk like that to a rank stranger.

The act of kind and timely speech over the lifetime of a marriage will make it or break it.

I close this chapter with a semi-happy ending on my lynx-slayer friend.

They did throw the book at him. He received a hefty fine, took his hunting rifle and four-wheeler (ouch), and was given a boatload of community service hours, most of which he did at Dry Creek Camp, where I served as manager.

The caveat of his sentence was, "You are forever banned from hunting in Colorado."

My friend shook his head. "There ain't *no way* I'm ever going back there, hunting or not."

He learned a lesson that he passed on to me, and I'm now passing on to you. Think before you act.

The impulsive life will be a troubled one. We laugh at what's called "A Redneck's Last Words," as in "Hey, y'all, watch this."

Sadly, I've had many friends who lived by that adage. Often, their lives were short, fast, and straight, ending in a vehicle crash, overdose, deep river, or the business end of a firearm.

Think before you act.

Take a deep breath before you shoot.

In every difficult situation, ask yourself, "Now, why would I want to go and do something stupid like that?"

It'll save you a ton of trouble.

Chapter 27

A Servant-Leader Named Jimmy

He was a servant-leader named Jimmy Barrett, and he helped shape my life.

Even now, eight years after his death, I cannot quite adequately explain his leadership style. All I know is he was a leader at East Beauregard High School for a generation of students and teachers.

He was an influence in my life at East Beauregard High School. He played significant roles as a teacher, driver's education instructor, principal, mentor, school board member, deputy, and, most importantly, friend.

I've been polling my East Beauregard High family about how they viewed Jimmy Barrett's personality and leadership.

His most significant influence on me was during his years as principal. I was under his leadership, first as a student and later as a young teacher/coach.

First of all, Jimmy Barrett liked people.

If you like people, they will like you.

He had a fine sense of humor and an easy-going manner that made people feel comfortable around him.

He also obviously cared about his students and teachers.

I don't care how much you know until I know how much you care.

Jimmy Barrett was extraordinarily humble, and genuine humility always attracts others.

Tragic events had touched him and shaped him as a man, resulting in a deep sense of empathy for others.

In Driver's Ed, he shared openly about the accident that changed him.

As a young teen driver, he accidentally backed over a small infant cousin killing him. In Driver's Ed he'd share about the accident. Each student was required to walk around the car before backing up.

Fifty years later, I still do that inspection. Many of my friends also still do it.

Mark Smith was my closest friend at East Beauregard. He and his brother Bob had lost their father as young teens. Jimmy Barrett picked the Smith brothers up each morning in the driver's ed car, teaching them to drive as they made the trip to school.

Mark said the best part was how Mr. Barrett talked with them, asking them about their lives and goals.

He had empathy and cared for those who needed extra attention, always looking out for the underdog.

I once thought of Jimmy Barrett's school leadership as *laissez-faire*

I'm not sure that was a fair assessment. He was definitely not a micromanager or control freak, but he was in charge. He did what I wished for as a classroom teacher: he got out of the way and let me do my job.

He had a rich, resonant voice that calmed people down. When he later served as a Beauregard Parish Sheriff's Deputy, I was with a group of children who asked him, "What's your best weapon?"

Jimmy Barrett smiled and opened his mouth. "My tongue. It's my best weapon. Many times, I'm able to defuse situations that lead to a peaceful resolve."

He later told me that Sheriff Bishop would send him on potentially volatile assignments.

I saw this same gentle spirit calm angry parents and lecture boys who were about to have fisticuffs by the lockers.

The boys cooled down. They understood what I knew:

You didn't want to disappoint him.

That is an overlooked asset of effective leaders. They have built trust, compassion, and respect with their team.

In return, they don't want to let their leader down.

I'd crawled on broken glass to Sugartown to avoid disappointing Jimmy Barrett. He inspired loyalty in his people. Amazingly, in one year, every single teacher on a faculty of over forty returned for the next school year.

He was unorthodox, and that's one of the reasons we loved him.

My friend Mike Gallien related this story,

"I was a senior and needed one-half credit to be eligible to play baseball that spring. I went to Mr. Barrett for help. He said, 'Mike, I'll design a course just for you. We'll call it 'News and Current Events.' During fifth hour every day, you'll go to the library and read every magazine and newspaper available.

"On Fridays, come to my office, and we'll spend an hour talking about the week's news."

Mike Gallien, who went on to be a highly successful principal, said, "I learned more in that weekly hour with Jimmy Barrett than probably any course I ever had. "

* * *

One of his nieces said it so well about Jimmy Barrett,

"Uncle Jimmy was gentle.

That gentleness did not demand respect—it earned it.

It did not drive people. It invited them.

It did not divide.

Rather, it brought people together."

His name was Jimmy Barrett, and he had an outsized influence on me for the first three decades of my life as a Dry Creek boy.

He was one of the quietest leaders I've ever known.

He was one of Dry Creek's great servant-leaders.

And that's one of the reasons we loved and revered him.

He was definitely a servant-leader.

He was, without a doubt, one of the most *unusually* effective leaders I've known.

I thought about Jimmy Barrett when I read the excellent book *Leaders Eat Last* by Simon Sinek.

The book's premise comes from the United States Marine tradition, which states that officers wait until the enlisted men are served.

As in "Leaders eat last."

The book is really about servant-leadership.

Throughout *Where I Come From*, I'll talk extensively about servant-leadership.

It's no accident that I've hyphenated the two stellar words: *Servant-Leaders.*

The most outstanding leaders I've known are servant-leaders. That's why we respect them, follow them, and love them.

It's a happy marriage: Servant-Leadership.

Even though *Leaders Eat Last* is a business leadership book, it's full of examples of the best leadership: servant leadership.

I thought about Jimmy Barrett as I was reading about Servant-Leadership.

It was the type of leadership that typified one of the most unique leaders I've known.

In a later chapter, we'll take a closer look at these concepts in *Leaders Eat Last.*

* * *

My sister Claudia related this story from her senior year:

Claudia's partner in crime, the one and only Kim Campbell, poked her head in the principal's office one morning.

"Mr. Barrett, I sure would like to go to town (DeRidder) today."

"Sure." He slid a sheaf of papers across his desk. "Since you're going, take these by the School Board Office."

"Well, Mr. Barrett. There's just one problem. I don't have a car."

Jimmy Barrett slid his keys across the desk. "Take my car. Just make sure you go by the School Board office.

Kim quickly rounded up her two co-conspirators, my sister Claudia and Linda Manuel, and they were off to "Town."

Ah, those were the days.

* * *

I close with my favorite Jimmy Barrett principal story.

One day, I was in the middle of a chemistry lesson when Jimmy Barrett slipped into the back of the classroom to observe me. No one noticed him but me.

He got comfortable. Mr. Barrett always looked sleepy, and soon, he began leaning on his elbow.

I thought. *This is too good to be true.*

I'd set up a chemistry experiment to demonstrate that two simple chemicals can have dramatic reactions when mixed. I had a short piece of 2 x 4 on my desk. I'd mixed a dab of potassium chlorate and manganese oxide on the board.

Before picking up my hammer, I glanced to the back of the classroom. Mr. Barrett seemed very relaxed, if not asleep.

I even waited a few minutes until I was sure he was out.

As I told you: *this is too good to be true.*

It had always been one of my favorite tricks. When I used it, I felt more like an ancient alchemist or wizard than a modern chemistry teacher.

I struck the mixture with the hammer.

An explosion went off as loud as a firecracker, and smoke boiled from under my hammer.

WHAM!

The students jumped a boy by the window cussed out loud.

They'd all been taken by surprise.

But my eyes weren't on my students. The loud crack jolted Jimmy Barrett awake. I thought he was going to tear that small wooden desk apart trying to get out.

I laughed as loud as I've ever laughed. In fact, I'm laughing as I write.

The students turned, and although they'd not had the ringside view I had, they joined in the good-natured fun.

Jimmy Barrett stood, grinning sheepishly.

I never let him forget it.

The best part was how he told the story over and over on himself.

That was another sign of why he was a good leader: he didn't take himself too seriously. He had a wonderful redeemable quality: he could laugh at himself.

I still chuckle about the "Firecracker in Room 13."

Nowadays, you'd have an active shooter alert and total lockdown, plus I'd have some explaining to do.

As I said earlier, those were the days.

* * *

When Jimmy Barrett died, I was honored to deliver his eulogy.

There were so many stories to tell concerning his basic kindness and caring for others.

From experience, I've learned that you should never tell a joke or a funny story at a funeral. But this was different: this was Jimmy Barrett's funeral. After getting his family's permission, I told the "Firecracker in Room 13" story.

Of course, it brought the house down. One retired teacher in the third pew laughed so hard I thought we were going to need to use the Heimlich maneuver on her.

It was a shame Jimmy wasn't there to share in the laughter. He would've laughed loudest of all.

But that story wasn't why I was up there. It was my chance to share the many qualities of my friend you've read above, such as his compassion, empathy, and genuine kindness.

Yes, Jimmy Barrett was my principal.

Best of all, he was my friend.

Chapter 28

The Fire

I can still see the sadness on Daddy's face as we stood over the fire-swept field.

It was the winter of 1964. All of the young pines were gone—burned to a crisp by a wildfire.

The previous year, Daddy and Uncle Bill had spent several weekends planting a portion of his forty acres in slash pines. I was eight and tagged along, tugging a sack of pine seedlings, trying to keep up as they planted.

The fire had taken it all. Not one pine survived.

Daddy was always stoic in times of trouble. He stood in silence over the ruins.

I never heard him ever mention the pines again.

He didn't bother to replant. Woods fires were too common in the era of open range and no fire lines.

* * *

Woods fires aren't the only reason for a barren field. Clearcuts are another. I've always had a love-hate relationship with clear-cuts. It breaks my heart to see the desolate landscape of broken pine tops and stumps as far as the eye can see.

A field after a clearcut looks like a photograph of no man's land from the First World War. Splintered trees. Broken bodies. Broken trees. Stumps where tall pines stood a week ago.

However, I've lived my life in the Pineywoods and understand this cycle of life and death.

Within a year, after burning the field, a planting crew will come in and plant pine seedlings in a rectangular grid of 8 x 10. That's one seedling every eight feet on a row and ten feet between rows.

If you have a room full of foresters and bring up the subject of spacing on planting pines, you'll be in danger of sparking a chair-throwing, window-breaking fistfight.

That's how strongly foresters of all eras and backgrounds feel about planting pines.

* * *

There's nothing I love more than watching a young stand of pines peeking above the weeds until they grow toward maturity.

These pines are planted to be harvested. That's why these vast fields are called pine plantations.

I'm not a forester, but I've studied the life cycle of pine plantations for my entire life. My home parish of Beauregard is covered by thousands of acres of growing pine stands.

After the twelfth year, the pines will be thinned by every fifth row. The remaining rows will grow faster as their canopies are exposed to more sunlight.

One veteran forester said, "Those pines need some elbow room."

In a dozen years, a second thinning will occur.

A succession of thinnings continues until a scattered stand of tall pines remains. At maturity, all of the remaining pines will be harvested, leaving a clearcut,

Then, the cycle of life begins again. That's why trees are called a renewable resource.

Although a clearcut hurts my heart, the timber industry drives our economy in Beauregard Parish. From the smallest pulp-wood operator to our large sawmill and paper mill, money does grow on trees.

However, I still have a mixture of emotions when I see a clearcut.

I recall my Dad's words after a large clearcut adjacent to his house: "Well, I know I'll never see big pines in that field again."

He was right. It was soon after the clearcut that my father died.

Each time when I looked over the desolate cutover, I was reminded of the barren spot in my heart due to the loss of this remarkable man I called "Daddy."

* * *

However, it's incredible how tall pines grow in two decades. The empty field is now a thick and healthy stand of pines. The trees are twenty years old because they were planted shortly after Daddy's death.

I'll remember how my Dad's death coincided with their new life. The stand of pines remains a measuring stick for me in the loss of my Daddy.

Man, I still miss him as much as the day he died.

Twenty years is such a long time.

At the same time, twenty years flashes by in a blink.

I sit at Mom's kitchen table, looking out the window at the thick stand of trees.

Yes, the joys of memory . . . visible in a field of tall pines.

Postscript

Replanting: The Longleafs

Maybe that's why, nearly fifty years after the fire, I replanted that same patch of land with pine seedlings.

I wanted to put it back in pines.

I didn't choose the slash pine seedlings Daddy planted years ago. I chose longleaf pines, the native fire-resistant tree of the Louisiana Pineywoods.

Longleaf pines are the natural trees of the Pineywoods. Before the Europeans came, they stretched in a broad band from southern Virginia to east Texas.

Their unique characteristic is that they not only survive wood fires but also thrive on them. In fact, a longleaf needs periodic fires to reach its potential.

I could preach a sermon about that. In fact, I have.

There's such a strong spiritual connection between fires and growth,

It's true with the longleafs.

It's also true with each of us.

Some of my pines are now twenty feet high. Others are still in the grassy stage.

I love being on my land when a strong north wind is blowing. The young trees shimmer and sway. If you listen closely enough, you can hear a whisper in the pines.

I wish Daddy could see that.

Maybe he has.

* * *

"They took all the trees

And put them in a tree museum,

Charged a dollar and a half just to see 'em.

Don't it always seem to go

That you don't know what you got 'til it's gone?

They paved paradise and put up a parking lot."

— *"Big Yellow Taxi"*

Joni Mitchell

Chapter 29

Where Everyone's Your Uncle or Aunt

I grew up in a great place—the rural South. There were so many wonderful things about a country upbringing, one of the best parts being the large extended family in which I was raised.

As a small boy, I had a multitude of great-grandparents, grandparents, great-uncles and aunts galore, and cousins,

In addition to my blood kin, I grew up with something else unique—a whole host of older adults who served as surrogate grandparents.

Most of these were addressed by the time-honored Southern title of "uncle" or "aunt." I'd probably started school before I realized most of them weren't really blood kin.

I could never figure out at what age, how it was decided when, and who would be known in the Dry Creek community as "Uncle Johnny" or "Aunt Alice." Not every older person received this honorific title; instead, it was reserved for those kind souls who seemed to exist everywhere in our community.

It was a title of endearment and, most of all, a term of respect. The younger people of our community always honored those we addressed as uncles and aunts.

I grew up in a rural community where it seemed every adult was my *uncle* or *aunt*. Although they appeared to be kin, I knew they couldn't all be kin.

They're two of the sweetest words in the English language:

Uncle.

Aunt.

In Dry Creek, these terms of respect were given to our elders. I knew them as Aunt Mary Jane, Uncle Jesse and Aunt Bessie, Uncle Tom and Aunt Jessie, and dozens more.

They're all gone except in my memory.

These folks reached their big arms and hearts around us with love, and that's how they became everyone's uncle and aunt.

China

I've found that these terms of endearment and respect aren't limited to our culture.

About twenty years ago, I went on a backpacking mission trip to China. It was unforgettable, as four of us hiked through remote areas, hiding copies of "The Jesus Film" in the local dialect. We'd drop off our packets in cornfields and under sacks of grain. Our goal was that each packet would be discovered after we'd been gone. We called this spreading the Gospel "Johnny Appleseed Style" sowing.

As in, "If you see dirt, throw seed."

We had no guide, and learning any Mandarin words was difficult. Our phrase-book was of little use.

Earlier on our trek, we met a younger man who spoke English. He explained the terms of respect for the rural Chinese. He said, "It is important how you speak to older women. Your greeting will often determine how you're greeted in a village or home.

"The Mandarin word for aunt is *Ayi*. It's pronounced "eye-e." It's used toward an older woman of grandmotherly age and means 'Respected aunt.'

"Ayi. It's Chinese for aunt.

"It was even stronger than that.

"It is respected aunt; honored aunt."

Ayi.

Our new friend explained, "China is in the second generation of its one-child policy, and an unintended side effect has been the disappearance of uncles and aunts.

"That's why it's such an important word to us. Ayi is an even stronger than your English 'aunt.'

This saddened me. This inopportune policy resulted in a tear of the fabric on which Chinese culture was built.

From that moment on, hiding the "Jesus Film" continued as our priority, but I also began looking for those older women.

Traveling through this rural area of SE China, we encountered rural citizens whom I suspect had never seen a non-Chinese face. Some of the older people would shuffle away at the sight of scruffy white backpackers coming around the corner of their house, and babies would often burst out crying.

Others would stand in startled silence.

I'd look for those older women with a smile, a nod, and a respectful "Ayi."

My Southern-English-Mandarin dialect was poor, but their smiles testified I'd gotten through. I discovered that one simple word was all the introduction needed.

Ayi.

There's probably a similar term of respect wherever you travel in the world. Every culture has terms of endearment that mean so much more than just words.

Ayi. I hope I never forget that word.

* * *

Here is a passage from Lonely Planet's *The Mandarin Phrasebook:*

"China's efforts to limit its vast population through their 'one child' policy is rendering several kin terms obsolete. Most Chinese no longer have uncles or aunts in the People's Republic, and the array of words for the extended family is on the endangered list."

Africa

My Ugandan friend, Joseph Anyovi, lives in the middle of a grove of thatched huts.

It's the family compound. During our stay, dozens of family members and kin poured in and out, all stopping to give a greeting as Joseph explained who each person was.

I was trying to sort out who really was a brother, sister, child, uncle, nephew, father, or aunt.

"Joseph, you introduced me to three different men as your father."

"They all are my fathers. They're the brothers of my parents."
"What about the two dozen you introduced as brothers and sisters?"

"You would call them cousins. We call them brothers and sisters."

I began sorting out the siblings with, "Same father? Same mother?"

This untangled the family tree— somewhat.

There was one group I was most anxious to meet: the Mzees in Joseph's clan. They were easy to spot: old, wizened men sitting outside on a log, puffing on pipes as they took in the busyness of their compound.

These uncles, grandfathers, or whoever are treated with the utmost respect. Joseph explains the term *Mzee* to me. It seems to be a more robust version of *Uncle or Elder.*

Mzee.

When I arrived in Africa in 2013, I was nearing sixty and had the standard gray of an American my age. My short salt-and-pepper beard had turned to mostly salt.

I guess that's how I became a Mzee.

I was an elder, but not elderly.

But in the war-torn, disease-ravaged South Sudanese border region, I was elderly. The average life span of a man is 55 years, so I was ancient in their eyes.

I became an uncle—a mzee.

They still call them that, and I accept it as a great honor,

* * *

Dry Creek

In this chapter, we've traveled from Dry Creek to rural China and northern Uganda, and we're back where we started.

Back home, we didn't refer to those remarkable men as *Mzees;* they were our uncles,

The nurturing women scattered along the creeks weren't called *A-ie;* They were our aunts.

Together, they helped mold and shape our lives.

I'm grateful for each one, and I'm thankful I grew up in a small community called Dry Creek, Louisiana.

A place where everyone was your uncle or aunt.

Chapter 30

A Lazy Man's Load

"I'm starting to see that that isn't me.
My freedom isn't free.
All I really want is some room to breathe.

Someday, I'll learn to say 'No!'
Find a way to lighten my load.
Learn to let go and say, 'No!'"

—"The Anthem of Mr. Dark"

The Arcadian Wild

I'm guilty of it. I have been guilty of it most of my life. That was proven again today when I was unloading my

work truck and trying to bring everything in the house in one load.

As I got in the kitchen, my iPhone slid out from my armload of books, papers, and mail. I knew I'd cracked the screen once it hit the tile floor.

I was trying to make one big load instead of two sensible loads, and I broke my iPhone. I had no one to blame but myself.

I was carrying a Lazy Man's Load. It tries to do too much at once, which often results in disasters like my drop.

One of my mentors, Mr. Jay Miller, had a unique way of saying he was over-loaded. "My wagon's wooded."

I knew exactly what he meant. I've been overloaded to the axles and understand how it feels.

If I could live my life over, I'd carry less Lazy Man Loads. I'd slow down some, not try to take or do everything.

I'd say *no* more while still saying *yes* to the things that really matter.

The myth of multi-tasking is just that—a myth. Our minds are made to focus on one thing at a time. In Western society, we pride ourselves on how many things we can (or try to) do at once.

I recently walked by a woman in the parking lot cradling four Walmart bags. One bag burst, and a bottle of wine fell to the pavement. As it shattered, I was amazed at how wide a splatter zone a broken bottle of wine can make.

I went to help the lady as she knelt beside the shards of glass. I offered to help, but she angrily waved me away.

I'm sure she was thinking about the futility of carrying a lazy man's load . . . or, in her case, a lazy woman's load.

We don't leave any room for margin in our lives. We must step away, and we'll return with a clearer picture.

A long-ago trip to The Appalachian Trail was my attempt to recreate that solitude in my life. I purposely went solo. I needed time alone in nature, walking in the mountains, and getting in touch with the Lord.

On about the third day of the trip, as my mind untangled and thoughts flowed, I prayed, "Lord, I want to feel your presence more on this trip. I need to pray more."

In my heart of hearts, I believe God's Spirit said, "Then why don't you just shut up, walk, and listen."

Maybe that wasn't the Holy Spirit's exact words, but I got the gist of it.

I was reminded that prayer isn't me doing all of the talking. It's also about listening, and that's what I did for the remainder of the trip. I listened, looked, and felt God's presence in everything around me.

It was simply wonderful.

I came back more determined than ever to balance my life and listen.

* * *

Going back to my Lazy Man's Load theme, the excellent book *Essentialism* by Greg McKeown has the theme of "Less is Better." It's a book I return to again and again.

Everything in our 21st-century society encourages us to carry a lazy man's load. To cram in too much.

The simplified life is the best life, but it takes hard work and discipline.

* * *

The most important work in unloading a wooded wagon is "No."

I read a quote from a successful businessman, "Many of the most important decisions I've made involved saying 'No.'"

It's easy to say no when you have a burning yes inside. That's why a written life statement with your values and goals is essential. I try to read my Life Statement, Seven Words, and Heart List daily. This serves as both a mirror and an inner compass in my life.

That daily *reflection* is an opportunity to compare my heart-list as I make decisions to say yes or no.

If it matches my values and moves me toward my goals, I can say yes.

If it doesn't, I'll politely say no."

Say no so you can say yes more often.

* * *

I love Dolly Parton's singing as well as her self-effacing humor. Dolly was singing "Jolene" on a variety show when her bodice unexpectedly split.

Dolly never missed a beat. "Well, that's what happens when you try to put fifty pounds of mud in a thirty-pound sack."

Dolly, in her east Tennessee drawl, was describing, in her ample way, about carrying a lazy man's load.

"Jolene, Jolene. Please don't take my man.

Please don't take him just because you can."

I have a confession to make. I don't always practice what I preach.

Yesterday, I brought in an armload of soft drinks from the truck. A single twelve oz. bottle of Coke fell to the floor and rolled under the table.

There's nothing better than a cold, fizzy Coca-Cola and how it burns going down. I love that fizz and burn. I often tell DeDe I'm drinking a medicinal Coke. I only mean it in half-jest.

And there's nothing as disappointing as a flat Coke.

And when you drop or shake a Coke, you'll have a flat Coke that foams like crazy when opened but is flat.

Life is too short to drink flat Coke.

Well, I didn't say I've got it all figured out, but I can promise you that I'm trying.

I'm really trying.

Chapter 31

Clayton Iles Road

"You'd better choose your rut carefully because you'll be in it for the next mile."

I grew up on a one-mile stretch of dead-end dirt road.

Notice I said dirt. That's different than gravel.

The quote above is only half-joking. Choosing your rut carefully was a part of my upbringing.

Our home and the Old House were the only ones at the dead end.

If we heard a car coming, they were coming to see us or lost.

It was only after moving away that I grasped the uniqueness of growing up in the only house at the dead end.

Later, they put gravel on the worst parts of the road. It was still an adventure.

Our hilly Louisiana road was lined with pine forests on each side. As a young boy, I spent many hours walking and riding my bicycle on this road. Later, as a teenager, I would take nighttime walks on this road. As I walked under the stars, the only sounds would be the crunching of gravel underfoot. The sound of gravel crunching under your feet is good for thinking, as is the sound of the wind in the pines and other nighttime noises—crickets chirping, frogs singing, and occasionally the cry of geese flying overhead.

In the days before 911 and green road signs, our road had multiple names. Our road didn't have a particular name. Adventuresome guests were told, "After you cross the narrow bridge, we're the next road on the right past the house with the windmill."

Daddy would add, "Don't give up. We're the house at the mile-long dead end.

Years later, the new 911 system required names for every road; ours became Clayton Iles Road.

Dad and Mom lived at 622 Clayton Iles Road. Mom still does.

* * *

There are still benchmarks for my life on Clayton Iles Road. A *benchmark* is a permanent marker from which points of reference are made. It indicates elevation and serves as a reference for surveys and tidal observations.

I grew up in a surveying family. Benchmarks were concrete markers set in the ground with a brass cap indicating the elevation. Most benchmarks were located near roadways.

They were essential in helping a road surveyor obtain a precise measurement to begin laying the foundation for a road's construction.

In my life, there are dozens of benchmarks along Clayton Iles Road.

The following is a major life-changing *benchmark* that took place on Clayton Iles Road:

My teenage nighttime walks were times of solitude. As I looked up into the clear night sky, thousands of stars were visible. Gazing at the vast field of glittering stars, one thought always hit me: "How can anyone not believe in God when they look into the night sky?"

Many times, I took my nighttime walk to mull over a decision or pray about a problem. One particular instance still stands out in my mind:

I had no major during my first year of college, and I was still unsure of what career decision to make. I'd reached the point where I had to choose an area of concentration and knew this was a life-altering decision.

As a nineteen-year-old young man, I was overwhelmed by the magnitude of this decision. I was standing on my road of life with several forks in the pathway ahead.

It was time to choose the path forward,

I also wanted God's will in my life. If only He would show me, I would be willing to follow.

On Christmas break, I was walking on our gravel road, mulling my decision.

As I walked along, it was a cold and clear winter night. The stars shone brightly, as they only can on a clear, moonless country night.

I hadn't brought a flashlight, and the snakes were in hibernation. As I walked along in the dim starlight, each step was one of faith.

As I walked, I prayed about my career decision. Here was my simple prayer: "Lord, guide me. Show me what you want me to do."

Then, in the quietness of the moment, God spoke to me. Not in an audible voice, but deep down in my heart—right where He speaks most clearly:

As you walk down this gravel road, you cannot see to the end of it. However, by taking one step at a time in the darkness, you will reach the end. There is just enough light for each step—no more, no less.

I realized that God was not going to lay out His plan for my entire life or even for the next five years. He would instead wisely lead me step by step . . . moment by moment. My responsibility was to take it one step at a time using the light I had.

I didn't have to see all the way to the end of the road to take one step. God knew my life's road all the way to the end, and He would guide me without fail.

This "enlightening" experience on a dark gravel road helped guide the decisions I needed to make as a 19-year-old. A lifetime and many careers later, God is still, when I listen, willing to give the guidance I need—one step at a time.

At some point in the late nineties, the police jury paved our road. I cannot overestimate what a big deal it was. I stood in the yard with Daddy as he said, "I never thought I'd live long enough to see our road paved."

We laughed.

He saw it, but not for long.

Within five years, he was gone, One more victim of Big C.

That's what I call cancer—big C. I think of some unprintable words to describe cancer.

However, I still think of Daddy when I travel on the road that bears his name.

* * *

A good name is rather to be chosen than great riches and loving favour rather than silver and gold.

—Proverbs 22:1

* * *

The front cover of *Where I Come From* is an early morning photo of Clayton Iles Road.

Chapter 32

The Catfish Lunch

I f you're going to understand the culture of Dry Creek Baptist Camp, you'll need to know about the monthly Catfish Lunch.

If you've read any of my thirteen books, you know I grew up in a unique place: Dry Creek doesn't even have a caution light, but we possess a deep sense of community, history, and connection with the land.

Dry Creek Baptist Camp is the center of the solar system in my hometown. The entire community depends on the Camp, and there is a positive feeling that everyone is part of the Camp family.

That's exactly how it should be.

* * *

The monthly Dry Creek Camp Catfish lunch is a sight not to be missed. Today, over two hundred hungry adults will line up for all-you-can-eat freshly fried catfish.

I've eaten catfish all over the world and will put Dry Creek Camp catfish up against any.

Part of it is how they cut the filets thin and serve it hot and fried, but the real reason is the ambiance. Dry Creek Baptist Camp is one of the most beautiful retreat centers in the country.

However, buildings aren't what makes the Camp (and the catfish lunch) unique.

It's the people, and the catfish lunch is a good example. Mix in several hundred hungry (primarily senior) adults, hot fried catfish served by the friendly camp staff, followed by good music, and magic takes place for twelve dollars per plate.

I've worked at Dry Creek Camp on and off since I was thirteen. From trash duty in 1969 to being manager from 1992 to 2006, it was one of the richest times of my life.

I never tired of hearing guests say, "When I drive through the gates, I feel God's presence."

It's a special place where people have been coming to sense God's presence for nearly one hundred years.

Humans can't create a special place like Dry Creek. Only God can, but a camp is where people can *come apart* and find rest—a welcoming atmosphere in a place where the distractions of life fade away.

If it sounds like I am bragging about Dry Creek Camp, I am. It's where God has worked the most in my life and where I always feel at home.

* * *

The Catfish Lunch is always a special day. Here's how it grew from its humble beginnings to what it is today.

The lunch started in the 1980s when Albert Hagan, my predecessor as camp manager, began the "Dry Creek Men's Luncheon." About a dozen or so of us would meet monthly in Dry Creek's dining hall in our rural all-male version of the Rotary Club.

The attendance grew slightly over the next several years until a steady twenty men gathered monthly.

Then, one month, Mrs. Kathleen Heard showed up. We didn't know it, but the earth was shaking under her feet, and things would never be the same.

Mrs. Kathleen was a tall, slim, elderly Southern Gentlewoman whom we all loved dearly.

Her husband, Barney, attended the Men's Luncheon monthly. Both were my distant cousins, so I can speak honestly:

Mr. B.T. "Barney" Heard was *overbearing* and especially domineering toward his subservient wife. I recalled my father-in-law's description of a pompous man he knew up in Catahoula Parish: "Curt, if you could buy him for what he's worth and sell him for what he thinks he's worth, you'd be a rich man."

That's how many Dry Creekers viewed B.T. Heard. *God rest his soul.*

But Dry Creek's view of Mrs. Kathleen was different. She was a sweetheart and deeply loved by one and all.

When they married in 1931, Mrs. Kathleen had just turned fifteen, and Mr. Barney was twenty-one. I've always surmised that her being a young teenager and their age difference shaped their marriage and relationship.

 So the day Mrs. Kathleen Heard walked into the Men's Luncheon and pulled out a chair, we were all surprised, none more so than her husband, Barney T. Heard.

Mrs. Kathleen had a trembling voice in the best of times, and today, it was shakier than ever as she took a seat at the table. "I had heard that *you men* have been having some good catfish, and I thought I'd join you."

I glanced at Mr. Barney, and the only word I could use to describe him was *agog*.

He was *agog,* as in the dictionary definition: "Wide opened mouth; agape; astonished; goggle-eyed."

Yes, that's the right word. Mr. Barney was agog. His mouth was open as if to speak, but no words came out.

.

* * *

That April day, Mrs. Kathleen Heard broke the glass ceiling and integrated the Men's Luncheon. She was the pioneer who opened the floodgates. Soon, other spouses showed up, followed by brave local women and more couples.

Then, the senior adults began attending. They arrived in dozens of church vans and buses, and the Community Catfish Lunch soon grew into what it is today.

Here's one thing to note: senior adults like to arrive early. Lunch is officially served at noon, but the attendees begin descending after ten o'clock.

On arrival, they began jockeying for choice tables by propping their chairs. I call this "Dry Creek musical chairs" and warn you: *don't mess with their reserved spots*. Certain church groups have had the same box seats for years.

There's the detectable murmur of fellowship. Every person in the dining hall is glad to be here.

A long line, with its own pecking order, jostles to get in the front of the line, which snakes around the room. They're lined up as if the Camp is going to run out of sweet tea and all-you-can-eat catfish.

At 11:30, they bless the meal early and then let them loose. I'd call it organized chaos, but it's a happy chaos.

There's nothing like a crowded room filled with clinking silverware, laughter, and good conversation. It's the sound of people enjoying being together, and it's hard to beat.

I call it "The sweet sound of Christian fellowship."

I ask Camp Manager Todd Burnaman, my son in the Lord, "Todd, how many are here today?"

"About 200."

"How many called in for a reservation?"

"Oh, about 150, Brother Curt."

We both laugh as I say, "That's about par for the course."

Over the years, we have tried everything to get people and groups to call in, but there are always about the same number of gatecrashers (I use that term in a sweet Christian spirit) instead of registrants.

We tried taking money at the door for one month, and it obviously irritated our guests and embarrassed our staff. I promised them never to do it again, so no one knows who put their money in the bucket. It's an honor system that seems to work well.

However, there's no problem if someone forgets to pay. Sometimes, a check for $1000 might arrive the week after the Catfish Lunch from one of last week's attendees. There will probably be a women's group at the Catfish Lunch that returns home and raises funds for scholarships to send ten kids to summer camp.

Honestly, the Camp has consistently lost money on the Catfish Lunch, but don't feel bad for them. The goodwill, P.R., friendships, and generous gifts are worth a million dollars.

We learned that it's often difficult to add numbers accurately to God's balance sheet. God's economy is unique and sometimes hard to trace.

Dry Creek Camp is an example of *how you cannot outgive God.*

The Camp always prepares extra fish and potatoes.

The two fish and five loaves never run out. Nothing goes to waste—no twelve basketfuls of leftovers. Every piece of catfish is happily consumed.

Surveying the full dining hall of eager catfish consumers, I ease up beside Todd. "Don't forget. You have Mrs. Kathleen Heard to thank for this."

* * *

Enjoy the Dry Creek Catfish Lunch, but *please-please-please* don't show up without calling ahead.

If you don't, we might put Mrs. Kathleen Heard in charge of taking money at the door.

Chapter 33

The Talking Stick

I have his walking stick— the one he carried in the latter years of his life when I knew him best.

His name was Frank Iles, but our family knew him as "Pa." He was my great-grandfather and a major link to our family's past.

Pa's ancestors were among the first pioneers to settle No Man's Land. Both of his grandfathers fought in the Civil War. One had earlier escaped from Ireland as a stowaway, and the other was captured at Vicksburg and then paroled.

His initials, "FI," are carved on the worn handle of Pa's walking stick. It's not a very sturdy stick, but neither was Pa in the last ten years of his life.

Those were the years I knew him.

Pa spent those last years in his favorite rocking chair on the dogtrot porch at the Old House. His perch had a breeze from three directions, was always shady, and allowed him a birds-eye view of the front yard and barn, with Crooked Bayou Swamp as the backdrop.

During those latter years of his life, he was content to sit with a cup of coffee beside him, a Zane Grey paperback in his lap, and his walking stick across his knees.

He'd watch me play in the front yard, fighting Germans and digging for gold. From time to time, I'd join him on the porch.

I regret I didn't ask more questions.

I wish I'd have listened better.

I remember his tales of walking through the vast longleaf tracts before they were clear-cut and being one of the first students at the "Who'd-a-Thought-It" School.

A personal favorite was his story of being chased by a wild bull of the woods, a hump-backed brahman bull, as he sprinted for the safety of one of the few remaining standing trees in the clear-cuts. In my mind, I ran with him to the lone tree in the entire area.

In the Pineywoods, they were called *Bremer Bulls,* and if I saw one in the open range of my childhood, I ran like fire toward the lowest-limbed tree.

Pa had memorable stories from his years as a teacher and principal. Here was one story I always requested:

He was paddling an unruly Pineywoods boy. The student had loose strike-any-where matches in his back pocket. Pa's first whack lit the matches, and the second lick put them out. Pa said that smoke boiled out of the boy's pocket.

He had literally "set his" britches on fire."

I'm sure that tale (pun intended) and many others were embellished, but I believed them. I still have a strong visual image of smoke roiling from that boy's pocket.

He never set my britches on fire but made several observations that shaped my life. This was the most lasting impression:

One day, I threw a kicking, screaming fit in the yard, and Pa called me over. I can still hear his words, "Son, I can see that you've got a strong spirit in you. If you don't take control of it, it'll hurt you and cause you much trouble in your life."

That was all he said. He went back to his paperback, and I returned to playing. I'm sure he wondered if his oldest great-grandchild had heard a word.

I took his words to heart.

Pa, I'm still working on it.

I've tried to tame that strong, wild spirit and channel it for the good.

I removed Pa's walking stick from the Old House: like the house itself, the pos-sessions inside are suffering from the ravages of time. Our family has gradually removed the paintings, photos, and family keepsakes.

I took Pa's walking stick from its spot by the log room chimney. I'm only the temporary caretaker until one of my cousins or sisters wishes to borrow it.

Pa's rocker still sits in the same spot on the dogtrot porch. It's the centerpiece of my YouTube studio.

How it ended up being painted red is a story for another time. If you see me, ask about it.

* * *

Recently, I read that various cultures in Africa and the Pacific Northwest have a tradition called "The Talking Stick." The chief elder wields it at clan gatherings and calls the group to order by stamping the Talking Stick on the floor three times.

Everyone around the bonfire becomes quiet,

As long as the elder has the stick, no one else can speak.

As we say, he has the floor.

At some point, the Talking Stick is passed around, and each member must have the stick before speaking.

Each member strikes the Talking Stick on the ground and shares.

Clan members can only hold it once, allowing every member to speak, and no one person can monopolize the gathering. When you hand it off, you must be silent.

(I've been at my share of church business meetings where a talking stick would've been handy.)

The stick passes among the other elders while the younger members respectfully wait their turn.

Only the clan leader has the right to speak more than once, and he may end the meeting at his discretion.

* * *

Recently, we took an Iles Family Trip to a cabin at Toledo Bend. All seventeen members of the Curt and DeDe Iles clan gathered for a memorable weekend of swimming, eating, games, and good fellowship.

After SaturdaSaturday'sg meal, I called everyone together. DeDe and I sat on a couch, surrounded by our sons, their wives, and our nine grandchildren.

I brought out Pa's walking stick.

I told them the stories of Pa's walking stick as well as the tribal ritual of the Talking Stick.

"All right, everyone gets one chance with Pa's Talking Stick. No one will be forced to share, but everyone is welcome. Be careful not to stamp the stick too hard; it's thin and fragile.

The Talking Stick began its journey around the circle as our three sons and their wives spoke first. Then, one by one, my nine grandchildren took the talking stick.

It was *moving* beyond words; some shared a scripture while others commented on what they were grateful for.

Several of the grandsons fiddled nervously with the talking stick. DeDe and I later agreed that we expected it to snap at any moment. If one of them had broken it, it wouldn't be the end of the world. Grandchildren are much more precious than any wooden stick.

That's one thing I learned from my people: relationships always rule over things.

Finally, the Talking Stick returned to me—the elder of this clan. I sat the stick across my lap, looking into the faces of the people I love best, especially *the nine great-great-great grandchildren of Frank "Pa" Iles.* I wanted to take it all in.

Getting this group together in the future will be much more challenging. Two of the grandsons are high school seniors, and one branch of the family is moving to New Orleans.

It'll be different.

Different but good.

As I returned the Talking Stick to the truck, I stood in the darkness, recalling Pa in his rocker, walking stick across his lap, remembering his lessons and stories from the Old House at the dead end of Clayton Iles Road.

The spot where the open pine lands slope into the hardwoods of Crooked Bayou Swamp.

The place I come from.

"You better get back to the country 'cause 'cause that's where we all come from."

—"Standing on a Rock"

Ozark Mountain Daredevils

Chapter 34

Friends Who'll Stand By You

"And she's every friend I've had.

She's never failed to cut a trail

Whenever times are bad.

Oh, she's every friend I've ever had."

—"Every Girl"

The Turnpike Troubadours

* * *

"A man *who has* friends must himself be friendly, but there is a friend *who* sticks closer than a brother."

Proverbs 18:24

I f a man's got a true friend who'll stand by him, he's fortunate.

If he's got two, he is blessed.

There's one thing I've learned in this season of life: The best friends are old friends. Some of my best friends are still men I met as a small boy.

* * *

It was the worst night of our lives. DeDe and I sat in a darkened hospital surgical unit. It was in the early hours of the night.

Just hours ago, we sat in the stands cheering on our East Beauregard Trojans. Our son, Clint, ran a QB keeper before being tackled by two Merryville players. When Clint failed to get up, I knew something was wrong.

He'd suffered a severe hip dislocation. Two ambulance rides later, we sat in a Lake Charles hospital, worried about our son, worried about his future. The night was such a blurry fog. The doctors were honest enough to inform us that this could be a crippling injury.

At about 2:00 a.m., our friends Joe and Judy walked in. We had been neighbors and mostly dear friends since college. We'd raised our children together in Dry Creek.

I faintly recall some drink or fast food they'd brought.

But I'll never forget the sight of our dear friends coming to sit with us. I cannot recall anything they said.

I don't remember anything they did or said. I only know that they showed up.

I just know they were there.

And I'll never get over their kindness to DeDe and me on that long night.

That's what good friends do. They show up. I call it the ministry of presence.

It was being there.

I have a blurred mental photograph of Joe and Judy walking in.

It'll be there until the day I die,

Because that's what friends do. They show up.

Real friends show up in our hour of greatest need.

Today, Clint Iles is a forester and tramps through the pines, briars, and thickets daily.

He's a great husband to Amanda and a committed father to Jack, Sydney, and Ellen.

I'm so thankful for God's healing in his life.

* * *

Real friends show up, even between nations.

There's a touching story concerning Harry Hopkins, President Franklin Roosevelt's closest aide during the Second World War.

During the darkest days of the War, the President sent Hopkins on a fact-finding trip to Great Britain in 1940.

The following is excerpted from an excellent article* by author Christopher Hohlman:

"The Nazi war machine controlled most of Europe. Bombs rained down on London, and the entire country was preparing for an expected land invasion by the Germans.

"Harry Hopkins spent two weeks with Prime Minister Winston Churchill to assess the situation and report to President Roosevelt on what America could do to help our Ally.

"It was near the end of Hopkins' fact-finding mission. While in Glasgow, Scotland, Hopkins, Churchill, and their company moved to the Station Hotel, where they ate dinner together. Dr. Charles Wilson sat beside Hopkins.

"On the way back to London, Churchill's train stopped where he reviewed brigades of civilian volunteers such as firefighters, members of the Red Cross, and those working in the Air Raid Precautions Service (ARP) and the Women's Voluntary Service.

Churchill would stop to introduce Harry Hopkins as he reviewed the members of each organization.

"This proved to be too much for the shy Hopkins, who hid among the crowds of spectators gathered to see Churchill, but to no avail.

Each time he hid, Churchill would coax him out of the crowds, shouting, 'Harry, Harry, where are you?'

"Next, Hopkins, Churchill, and company moved to the Station Hotel, where they ate dinner with A member of Parliament, Tom Johnston. While at dinner, Dr. Charles Wilson sat beside Hopkins.

"Hopkins' disheveled and unkempt appearance struck Wilson; he looked worse than he ever had before.

"Invariably, the time for speeches arrived.

"When Hopkins' opportunity to speak came, he stood and began his speech by making a few jokes about the English Constitution and Churchill. Then, he turned to Churchill and said, 'I suppose you wish to know what I am going to say to President Roosevelt on my return.'

"Indeed, this was the moment Churchill had been waiting for; the fate of his entire nation hung on Hopkins' following words.

"'Well,' Hopkins continued, 'I'm going to quote you one verse from that Book of Books in the truth of which Mr. Johnston's mother and my own Scottish mother were brought up'—Hopkins lowered his voice to a whisper and quoting from the Book of Ruth said,

"'Whither thou goest, I will go; and where thou lodgest, I will lodge; thy people shall be my people, and thy God my God.'

"Then, Hopkins added his own personal touch to the beautiful verse, softly saying, 'Even to the end.'

"Churchill broke down in tears.

"Everyone present understood the significance of the words Hopkins had uttered.

"Dr. Charles Wilson wrote of the moment that, 'Even to us, the words seemed like a rope thrown to a drowning man.'

"President Roosevelt's man had spoken."

Once again, a friend standing by a friend in their time of greatest need.

Because that's what friends do, whether it's in London at the lowest point of the Second World War or a lonely ICU waiting room, you'll never forget friends who stand by you.

***

And Ruth said," Entreat me not to leave thee, or to return from following after thee: for whither thou goest, I will go; and where thou lodgest, I will lodge: thy people shall be my people, and thy God my God."

—Ruth 1:16 KJV

"Oh Brother,

What if I'm far from home?

Brother, I will hear you call.

What if I lose it all?

Oh, sister, I will help you out

Oh, if the sky comes falling down for you,

There's nothing in this world I wouldn't do for you."

—"Oh, Brother"

Avicii

* * *

*Harry Hopkins source: stmuscholars.org St. Mary's University. Dec 15, 2021 by Christopher Hohman

Chapter 35

Sleeping on the Ground

"Come to the woods, for here is rest."

—John Muir

* * *

"When you sleep on the ground
With the stars in your face,
You can feel the delight
Of its beauty and grace."

—Dan Fogelberg "The Wild Places"

I still cannot explain why I get this primal urge to sleep on the ground. I'm sixty-eight and should have more sense than to spend the night in the woods in a sleeping bag.

This crazy itch usually occurs in the Spring or Fall when temperature and humidity are lower. These have the best weather in Louisiana: cool nights with few mosquitoes and clear skies.

My last adventure took place on my land in Dry Creek. It was the end of March and a perfect night: cool enough to discourage the mosquitoes, a clear sky with low humidity, and no moon, so the stars would have their chance to show off.

I didn't bring a tent. I'm here to sleep under the night sky and want nothing to obscure the view.

I sat in my lawn chair beside a crackling campfire, watching dusk settle into darkness. This comforting fire gives a warm glow and drives off the last of the mosquitoes.

My Purple Martins are tucked in bed in their bird boxes on the levee.

My faithful dog, Bandit, is by my side.

It has the beginnings of a fine night.

I lay on top of my sleeping bag and scanned the southeast sky for the first star of the night. I watched for the brightest star, Sirius, the dog star, the heart of Canis Major. It's always the first star to appear; at this time of year, it is in the southeast sky. I strain to see the first stars of Canis' partner, the Hunter, Orion.

Faintly, I make out Orion's three-starred belt and then its red heart, the star Betelgeuse.

To the north, the big dipper continues its circle circuit around Polaris, the never-moving North Star. Behind me, low on the western skyline, the planet Jupiter makes its journey to set behind the treeline.

Nothing blocks out the stars, and they are stunning. The Milky Way stretches across the sky. Because Dry Creek is far from light pollution, this long band of stars and galaxies is stunning.

I hear the soft squeal call of a brace of late-arriving wood ducks, followed by their splash in my pond.

These dueling owls call off in the swamp. As the dueling barred owls continue their chatting, I detect a more excitable song at the end of their calls. I've got the best seat in the house. I've got a front-row box seat for the evening hoot owl concert.

In *Louisiana Birds,* Dr. George Lowery states, "Hoots are followed by a long-drawn-out weird scream that is enough to chill the bones of the uninitiated."

I agree with the spookiness of this scream. Owls have mocking, spooky calls that end with my nearby owl flying toward the west and the other owl flying to meet him. I recall that the prior generation of my people had a long list of superstitions and adages about owls.

It's darker now. I shudder as coyotes yip to the west in the swamp, encouraging me to get in my sleeping bag on the ground. It lies atop a sleeping pad and a blanket. I won't be cold. I'll be cozy.

The fire dies down, and I doze off. Bandit nuzzles beside me.

I woke up several times during the night. The entire night sky has changed. The wheel in the sky turned while I was asleep. Each time I awake, I observe the movement of the constellations due to the Earth's spin. I recall the Journey song "The Wheel in the Sky Keeps on Turning."

It's perfect weather—low humidity, cloudless sky—and the night sky shows off as only it can when city lights are absent.

The constellations from dusk have set, and a new host of friends is in the eastern sky.

The movement of the night sky ebbs at dawn. A nearby Red Cardinal wins the early bird of the morning award. His whistling song is my alarm clock. Soon, he is joined by other songbirds.

My bag is soaked with dew, my pad has slipped, and there is a layer of dirt on it.

However, I'm glad I slept in the woods on this star-lit night. Everything seems different as I walk through the woods to my mother's house for a fresh cup of coffee with her.

You ask why I sleep in the woods.

I answer, "Because I need to. "

Maybe because I *have* to.

What would make a man my age want to leave a warm, comfortable bed beside my wife and sleep in the woods on the ground?

I don't know.

I cannot fully understand it.

Tonight, I'll sleep in a warm bed with the woman I love.

I'll wake up to the smell of hot coffee brewing.

Those are good things and best appreciated after a night out.

A night sleeping on the ground.

In the wild places

Man is an unwelcome guest

But it's here that I'm found

And it's here I feel blessed.

—"In the Wild Places."

Dan Fogelberg

Chapter 36

Greg Johnson on Kindness

"There are three ways to ultimate success:

The first way is to be kind.

The second way is to be kind.

The third way is to be kind."

—Fred Rogers (Mister Rogers)

Greg Johnson is far and away the kindest person I know.

I first met him at a church meeting in the Ten Mile area. Todd Burnaman and I watched this short fellow sing, sway, and lead the singing from the front pew.

I told Todd, 'I don't know who he is, but we're taking him home with us."

That began the ongoing relationship between Dry Creek Baptist Camp and Greg Johnson. It took a while to convince his parents, Vance and Evelyn Johnson, that we could be trusted with Greg at the Camp. He quickly became a fixture at the Camp year-round, including summer camps.

Some people would say that Greg is simple.

Simple? Yes.

Greg has distilled life into two simple mantras: *Love God and love people*. He has put into practice what Jesus called "The Two Greatest Commandments,"

"Jesus said to him, 'You shall love the Lord your God with all your heart, with all your soul, and with all your mind. This is *the* first and greatest commandment. And *the* second *is* like it: 'You shall love your neighbor as yourself."

Greg's got those two-down pat.

Some might describe him as special.

You bet. Greg is special. Very special.

He affects everyone he comes into contact with.

If that isn't special, what is?

Greg has the kindest spirit I've ever known.

He also has a pure heart.

He'd be just as comfortable in the Oval Office as at the fifth Sunday Singing at Occupy #1 Baptist Church.

Greg is that way. He's comfortable in his own skin, and that's a compliment to any man, and that's a good way to describe a man.

Greg describes himself very well, "You know, Brother Curt, I'm handicapped."

I smile. "Greg, I've seen some people who were truly handicapped in their soul and heart, but not you."

Each time I'm with him, I learn something from him.

No pretense. No show. Just himself.

I've always loved Pineywoods men like that. *What you see is what you get.*

* * *

The following stories exemplify Greg's *kindness and spiritual awareness*, which often travel hand in hand.

I don't think spiritual awareness can be taught. It's a God-given gift.

When I was Camp Manager at Dry Creek, Greg spent most of the summer with us.

One of our summer staffers, Tiffany, received a call on the kitchen phone that her grandfather had died.

As she wept, the other staffers encircled her in love.

I stood back, watching. Here, I was the supposedly spiritual leader of this group, and I had no idea what to say or do.

Someone bumped me as he passed by. It was Greg. He wiggled through the circle of staffers, hugging Tiffany as he prayed a simple, heartfelt prayer.

I thought. I am in the presence of someone spiritually far greater than me.

* * *

Greg has a deep desire to read the Word.

"Brother Curt, when I get to Heaven, I'll be able to read."

"Greg, I believe that. I believe it with all of my heart."

It's amazing what a special friend can teach us. Greg has been my teacher in so many ways. I am privileged to call Greg Johnson a dear friend.

* * *

A Few Parting Shots on Kindness

I've spent most of my life gathering stories and quotes on kindness. Before leaving the subject, I'd like to leave you with a bushel basket of good quotes on kindness:

Kindness is not a weakness.

The world often dismisses proffered kindness as naive. I believe kindness is one of life's greatest assets. It's an investment that grows inside you as you give it away.

It's a trait that both blesses the receiver and the giver. It leaves both with a spring in their step.

Always be kind, and always be kinder than necessary.

Kindness is a language the blind can see and the deaf can hear. It's a language anyone can understand.

Kindness is one of the best words in the English language.

Kindness. It's a fine word. It's a Jesus-kind of Word.

Kindness. It's a word I want to use in my vocabulary and show in my life.

The opposite of kindness is rudeness. There is no room for rudeness if your heart is full of gratitude and kindness.

A tenet of good Southern hospitality is to speak and act with kindness.

If you can be anything, be kind.

"Constant kindness can accomplish much. As the sun makes ice melt, kindness causes misunderstanding, mistrust, and hostility to evaporate."

—Albert Schweitzer.

"Kindness makes a man attractive."

—Proverbs 19:22 (The Living Bible)

Chapter 37

Saying Goodbye to a Grand Old Lady

T hroughout my life in Dry Creek, a building has stood that served not only as a link to the past but also as an anchor for our community.

It was known as "The Dry Creek White House," had a personality of its own, and was also known as "The Grand Old Lady."

Originally built during the years surrounding World War I, it served as our local school from its construction until its closure in 1962. The men of the community built it over nearly a decade, and they constructed it sturdily and with great care.

Over the years, we've discussed the style in which the building was constructed. When I posted a photo of the building on Facebook, folks came out of the woodwork (pun intended) with everything from antebellum to colonial to plantation style. I will say it was unique.

The Dry Creek (DC White House) clearly had some of the paladin neo-classical structure of the south façade of the other DC (as in the District of Columbia) White House.

Another fact is that the Dry Creek White House was initially painted brown.

After its years as Dry Creek High School, it remained vacant for the next two decades. A family from Minnesota bought it as a winter home, but they didn't use it much. We always said it was too cold inside, even for Northerners.

Amazingly, during these empty years, there was no vandalism or broken windows. That shows the community loved this building.

Later, Dry Creek Baptist Camp bought the Old School and renovated it into a bed-and-breakfast-style building with twenty-seven lodging rooms.

Although its official name became the Adult Conference Center (ACC), it was affectionately known as the "Dry Creek White House." For the next four decades, it hosted hundreds of events and thousands of guests.

It was such an exciting facility: two stories with 14-foot-high ceilings and rooms of every size and shape. During my fourteen years as camp manager, I had the privilege of watching God change so many lives within its walls.

Unlike most rural schools that closed during the 20th century, it wasn't torn down or allowed to deteriorate over the years. It was given a new lease on life as part of the Camp.

Its use as a facility ended on Wednesday, February 17, 2021, when it burned to the ground. As sad as I am at the loss of the White House, I'm glad it didn't rot down or be unceremoniously hauled off piece by piece. Dry Creek Camp gave it a reincarnation of continuing to serve our community and thousands of guests.

Let me get this out of the way: some folks called this building a "White Elephant." It was expensive to renovate, causing the Camp to take on an enormous debt at a time of high inflation.

Admittedly, it wasn't easy to maintain, nor was it easy to heat and cool. When someone said it was a white elephant, I'd smile and reply,

"Yes, it may be a white elephant, but it's *our* white elephant."

I used the term "our" on purpose. Although Dry Creek Camp owned the White House, the entire community felt it belonged to them and loved it like the grand old lady it was. It seemed as if everyone in Dry Creek had a story about how the White House had touched their lives.

Camp Manager Todd Burnaman described countless people sharing in person or online after the fire about the building's place in their lives.

They spoke of wedding receptions, how far the school bell could be heard, voting there in local elections, and kids running up and down the carpeted stairs on each end of the White House.

Sam Burchard, pastor of Dry Creek Bible Church and next-door neighbor to the White House, said it so well, "I feel as if we should have a funeral."

It was as if this building were a personal friend and the anchor of our community. Yes, a funeral for a Grand Old Lady might have been appropriate.

Last week, when I stopped by the ruins of the White House, someone had placed a vase of colorful flowers on each step. It was someone's heart-felt action that a beloved object was gone.

I never attended DryCreek High School, beginning in first grade the year after it closed. Even though the "new school" at East Beauregard was nice, I was still envious of the older students who told stories about the "Old School."

They bragged about climbing the stile during recess and walking Elliott'st's Grocery across the highway. Other stories included tales of sliding down the banisters and how many of the classes were combined because of its small enrollment.

If my memory is correct, fewer than four hundred students graduated from 1921–1962, an average of about ten per year. It was a small rural school, and they don't make them like that anymore.

Don't discount for a minute the quality of education these students received. Dry Creek graduates have excelled at every level of society.

My Dad always pointed out his first-grade classroom, which eventually became a large conference room. "I was in first grade in that corner., and the second graders were across the room. The teacher busily tag-teamed both grades. Daddy said that he listened to the second-grade lessons while doing seatwork. "The next year, when I moved across the room to second grade, I'd already heard it all."

Certain people are tied to my mind when I think about the White House. Here are several:

My mentor on the history of the old school building was Frank Miller. Mr. Frank, as we called him, had a unique distinction. He'd been a student, teacher, and principal at Dry Creek High. He loved the old building like the Grand Old Lady it was.

Mr. Frank showed me every inch of the Old School and seemingly had a story for each step. I share my favorite in his own words:

"I was in elementary school when they finished school. The four hollow columns were hauled in by oxen-drawn wagons from the sawmill at Longville. They were laid down in front of the school and quickly became a recess favorite as the younger boys would crawl through the tunnel of the columns.

As this went on for weeks, some high school students played a prank. While several first-grade Dry Creekboys were in the tunnel, the older boys nailed planks over each end of the column. The trapped boys were not discovered and freed until their teacher came outside after recess and heard them crying and yelling."

As I said, Mr. Frank always had a story for every square foot of the Old School. I still miss him, but I am glad he wasn't here to see it burn to the ground.

A second person with a long history in the White House was Mrs. Eleanor Andrews, who faithfully taught elementary school there for two decades. Later, she was my fifth-grade teacher at East Beauregard. She became my favorite teacher, and we maintained a close friendship until her death.

Mrs. Eleanor lived by herself, not far from the old school. When she turned eighty, she begrudgingly permitted us to plan a birthday party. I insisted we have it at the White House.

She scoffed as she flicked ashes off her latest cigarette. "There won't be anybody to come see an old woman like me."

We planned the party in the coming weeks despite her skepticism. I'll never forget the sunny April Saturday of the party.

She sat in a chair as a steady procession of former students, friends, and lifetime neighbors paraded by with their well wishes. Her smile, as dozens of people kissed her, hugged her, and gave gifts, was touching.

When the party finally ended, she turned to me, pointing a bony finger in her stern teacher voice. "You know, I'm still mad at you for having this." Then she broke into the smile I loved so dearly. "But I so enjoyed this. Thank you."

That smile of this special person in the building, who was a big part of her life, is forever etched in my mind.

No fire or ashes can erase it. It'll always be my heart-snapshot memory when I think of the White House. In spite of the losses, I still smile, recalling that day.

Speaking of memories, so many photos, decorations, and mementos burned up. As I heard someone say, "Lots of pictures burned up when the White House burned down."

I often think of lost items that cannot be replaced. Does anyone have another photo of Dry Creek's famous 1931 state championship basketball team? How will we ever find another Dry Creek Hawks uniform top?

So many things are lost and gone forever.

As I inventory these losses, I think of another woman with a strong connection to the White House. Doris Pate Hennington attended school there, graduating with the last senior class. She met her husband, Roger, there, and when they returned to Dry Creek after retirement, Mrs. Doris took command of her old school building.

Mrs. Doris was in charge of cleaning the White House. She took pride in caring for the Grand Old Lady. It was her building, and if anything were amiss, she would immediately report and correct it. Her life was tied up in this building, and her work was a labor of love.

Doris Hennington is one of the first people I thought of when the fire occurred.

When she retired from the Camp, we presented Doris with a plaque commemorating her years of service. It hung in the old school's former principal's office among photographs, class lists, and newspaper clippings on the wall.

When the White House burned down on that cold February afternoon, everything burned up. No source for the fire has been clearly identified, and electricity and water were cut off to the building. We may never know what started the fire.

Visiting with manager Todd Burnaman a month after the fire, I expressed relief that, in spite of the great loss, no one was in the building when the fire happened. One of my nightmares as manager was the fear of the building burning while guests were present. We all knew that the rich lighter pine would burn like a torch if a fire ever started.

And that's precisely what happened when the White House burned down. Nothing was left except the steps and the school bell.

* * *

I've chosen to celebrate how God used this Grand Old Lady in both of her careers.

She spent over forty years as our community school. Then, after being abandoned for two decades, the White House received a facelift and a second life as a place where people enjoyed comfortable lodging, good food, and fellowship within her walls.

Its hallways will always echo laughing, pajama-clad ladies on Friday nights at women's retreats. They still hold the sound of my Aunt Margie Nell playing the piano to the delight of guests. She chews gum, tickles the ivories, and catches my eye with a wink and a smile.

In God's economy, the White House served its purpose well. It's gone now. Dry Creek Camp will build another adult facility in the future. Someone said they should "Build it just like the White House."

My reply was, "You couldn't build another White House even if you tried. And besides, the new building will be unique and modern, serving others."

I have one final story.

Each year, we hosted a couple's retreat at the White House. The private rooms with double beds and privacy were perfect for these marriage-enrichment events. The week before the event, a woman called wanting to reserve two rooms for the Friday-Saturday event. I carefully inquired, "You and your husband want separate rooms?"

She shared how they'd been separated for most of a year, the result of marital infidelity on his part. What she didn't say was something I picked up: this was a last-ditch effort to save a faltering marriage.

The couple arrived separately, and to say it was awkward would be an understatement. However, as I observed them throughout the weekend, I detected a thawing in their body language and communication. It was an excellent marriage enrichment led by a fine pastor and wife who taught and showed by example how to make a good marriage even better.

No one else knew about the separated couple. I sure didn't tell, but I prayed. When the couple left on Saturday afternoon, they had hope that maybe, just maybe, their marriage could be rebuilt.

The wife later sent a note that they had reconciled.

That story illustrates one of a multitude of lives changed by God at the Dry Creek White House.

They are all memories now. I'll always miss this special building. Like Mr. Frank Miller, Mrs. Eleanor Andrews, and Mrs. Doris Hennington, it played an outsized part in my life. I'm glad God let me in on what He was doing at Dry Creek.

Especially at a Grand Old Lady we called the White House.

Chapter 38

Bare-footing

"Brother Leeds? He *warn't* no Yankee. He was one of us."

—Pineywoods logger in Ouiska Chitto Swamp

circa 1900

The families working at the chimney raising stopped work to gawk.

It was Saturday in a small, secluded logging camp of the late 1890s.

Everyone stopped when the stranger rode into view.

They didn't see many outsiders here in the backwoods.

The men watched from their work, building the skeleton of limbs for the new chimney.

Several women stood from their boiling washpots. Even the children in the mud-daubing pit stopped stomping.

Someone whispered, "Look how he's dressed up. He must be that circuit-riding preacher we've heard-tale of."

You didn't see fellows like him deep in the Pineywoods.

An awkward silence ensued as the stranger tied his horse and walked towards the small, clannish group of pioneers.

In his memoir, *Patteran*, Reverend Paul Leeds described that day:

"I was from up North, and that definitely made it difficult. I was an outsider. Plus, being a man of the cloth, I was dressed differently and didn't fit in.

"But one Saturday, I found the key to reaching these rugged backwoodsmen. I chanced upon a chimney raising. I placed my coat on my saddle, rolled up my pant leg, and stepped into the mud daubing pit. We had a great time stomping that mud and straw. From that day on, that settlement treated me as one of their own."

Paul Leeds illustrated a key concept in building relationships.

It's called bare-footing.

Rev. Leeds was bare-footed—literally and figuratively. He got in there, mixed in, and made a connection that opened doors.

It's always about relationships. But isn't everything?

Relationships can start anywhere, even in a clay pit.

Rev. Leeds understood the importance of bare-footing, literally and figuratively. It means getting out among the people and walking with them through their lives.

In over fifty years of ministry from his base in Kinder, Paul Leeds left giant footprints in the Louisiana Pineywoods.

The woodsmen and their families of Paul Leeds' era were a hardy lot. The loggers lived in rough-hewn log cabins, and they were rough-hewn.

Transient men primarily populated the deep woods camps. However, some loggers and their families homesteaded land near navigable creeks and rivers.

These were rough, and they were tough people.

They lived outside the limits of society and disdained city living.

These are the people that Paul Leeds ministered to during his circuit riding years at the turn of the century.

The loggers cut the longleafs, dragged them to a stream, and then slid them in at places called dumps. Before building their rafts to go downriver, the loggers stamped their brands into the end of each log to ensure proper credit and cash for their logs.

The Calcasieu was the river used by foresters to transport log rafts to the mills on Lake Charles. Loggers started their floats in late spring when the river was high but within the banks, lessening the chance of snagging a raft.

After reaching Lake Charles, they'd sell their logs. Cash in hand, most of the loggers would buy a horse or mule, load some essential supplies, and begin their ride walk home. Others walked, not willing to pay for an additional animal to f eed.

Ten Mile merges with the Whiskey Chitto near Mittie, and the Whiskey Chitto then flows into the Calcasieu north of LeBlanc.

Among his many preaching points, Paul Leeds worked in the Barnes Creek and Dry Creek areas where my people were. Rev. Leeds performed the wedding of my great-grandparents, Frank Iles and Theodosia Wagnon.

Bare-footing in Africa

DeDe and I moved to Africa in 2013. For the next three mission years, we worked among unreached people groups who'd had little access to the Gospel. We were tasked with learning where they lived, what they believed, and how they could be reached.

Our assigned areas were northern Uganda and the new country of South Sudan.

Bare-footing was a concept drilled into us as African missionaries. You can't learn about an unreached people group from behind a desk, on a laptop, in a book, or from Google Earth or Wikipedia.

You've got to get out of the box and be among the people. Get out there and see it with your own two eyes.

You've got to go bare-footing. Get out among them.

Bare-footing was also called ground-truthing, as in *don't take anyone's word for it.* The African rumor mill spins just as fast as the American version.

Ground-truth it.

In our Pineywoods culture, we call it *seeing it with the naked eye.*

Ground-truthing.

It's basically what DeDe and I did for three years in East Africa. Our main job was to find and research unreached people groups in Northern Uganda and South Sudan.

To accomplish this, we traveled to the far reaches where the tribes lived. We sat among them, shared meals with them, and listened to their fascinating stories about their tribal origins, folk stories, and beliefs.

Both upcountry northern Uganda and its neighbor, the wild-west country of South Sudan, were challenging.

I quickly learned about the term *ground-truthing*. You don't believe any word of mouth until you've seen it with your eyes.

This means seeing it firsthand, not taking anyone else's word for it. You can't learn everything you need to know about a people group from a map, laptop, or Wikipedia.

You've got to get out there and ground-truth. Put your boots on the ground to see where people live, how they live, and what they believe.

Word of mouth is good, but it should always lead to ground-truthing.

* * *

Ground truthing among the Baby-Stealers

We'd been warned, "Stay away from the Murle. They are bad people. They steal babies."

No one had anything good to say about the Murle, an eastern Ugandan tribe. We were determined to learn the truth about these supposed evil baby-stealers.

I heard that a group of Murle were in a refugee camp near where we were working. As I spent time among them, I discovered that they were hospitable and open to our friendship. I didn't meet any baby-stealers.

It was an oft-repeated false prejudice from nearby tribes.

Sadly, I've traveled much of the world and found prejudice exists among every person, tribe, and race.

Then there were the Kakwa. All we knew was that they were a primarily Muslim people group located where the countries of Uganda, South Sudan, and Democratic Congo met. Their greatest claim was that Idi Amin, possibly Africa's worst dictator, was Kakwa.

We traveled with our missionary partners to Koboko, the Kakwa Ugandan homeland, to see for ourselves.

It was work getting to know the people and find evangelical leaders in Koboko. We began a warm partnership that lasted through our three years upcountry. Churches were planted, and pastors trained.

Best of all, when DeDe and I returned to the States, our home church, Dry Creek Baptist Church, adopted the Kakwa as their people group. The work continues in each of the three co-joining countries.

Our Louisiana team went ground-truthing and became bare-foot missionaries.

That's what ground-truthing is: going bare-foot among the people and seeing it with your own naked eye.

* * *

Bare-footing can be intimidating, even risky. You're entering a tribal area where many of the people are wary of any intruder, especially Whites. You're outside your world in unfamiliar territories.

But greeting people with a smile that is understood in any language. Sitting by their fires and eating in their huts, a connection occurs, and relationships are born.

Before sounding too brave, we always took an African with us who was conversant in a common language, and we always parked our Land Cruiser face out in case we needed to get out of Dodge.

We'd spend two weeks in the bush before returning to our Ugandan home in Entebbe. We'd rest, recharge, reload, write our reports, then hit the road again.

It was a time we'll never forget. We were bare-footing.

Out among people vastly different from us.

Many were suspicious of us until they got to know us, and we got to know them.

We shared their food and huts. We listened to their stories.

They accepted us into their huts and hearts.

The men paraded us through the village, holding my hand.

The women gathered around DeDe, sharing in the warm connection that bonds women all over the world.

They didn't say, "He warn't' no Yankee. He's one of us," but I hope they said it behind our backs in Swahili, Dinka, or Nuer.

Get out there.

See it.

Get your boots on the ground.

Go bare-foot. So you can feel the soil.

It's the key to building relationships.

It's the key to growing relationships.

Be out there with the people, where someone will say, "Look at him; he's a bare-foot follower of Jesus."

But nothing is quite like going "bare-footing. Going there and putting your bare feet, or in our case, boots, on the ground. Getting in among the people and seeing, feeling, and tasting.

Get out there.

I believe Bro. Leeds would've liked that.

* * *

Postscript

I highly recommend *The Life and Times of Paul Leeds:*

The Apostle to the Pineywoods

by Katherine Johnson and Paul Leeds

www.wisepublications.biz

* * *

In his notes, Reverend Leeds used so many unique terms familiar to the Piney-woods of his era:

He wrote of being caught in the woods by nightfall, "I made a hog bed for the night," a Pineywoods term for sleeping on a bed of pine straw.

He described walking through the woods during a rainstorm, "My natural roof leaked."

Reverand Leeds often traveled between his circuits on foot. He described one such trip, "I took nature's carriage to reach the next hamlet."

Chapter 39

Leaders Eat Last

Thoughts on Servant-Leadership

"For even the Son of Man did not come to be served, but to serve, and to give His life as a ransom for many."

-Jesus in Mark 10:45

Earlier, I mentioned a fascinating book by Simon Sinek, *Leaders Eat Last*. The book's premise is based on the United States Marine tradition of officers waiting until the enlisted men are served.

Leaders eat last.

I've been fascinated with leadership my entire adult life. It's a subject that shapes families, organizations, sports teams, and even countries. Effective leadership is difficult to define, but suffice it to say that when you see good leadership, you know it.

Conversely, poor leadership is hard to miss, too.

Authentic leadership is not some boss or head honcho lording it over others. Good leadership is inevitably about servant leadership.

As in, leaders eat last.

A true leader puts the team ahead of themselves. This results in a connection and commitment where the team will follow that leader anywhere.

It's servant-leadership.

* * *

I recently read a deeply touching passage from *Martin Gilbert's The History of Israel*. The setting is the 1948 Israeli-Arab War.

During a heated battle, superior Arab forces were overrunning an Israeli platoon when their leader, Simon Alfasi, issued an order, "All privates will retreat while commanders give covering fire.

The enlisted men escaped to safety. Captain Alfasi and his fellow officers were killed while protecting their comrades.

His order, *"All privates will retreat—commanders will give covering fire,"* became the watchword for the young Israeli army.

It still is to this day.

Privates to the rear—commanders give covering fire. That's servant-leadership in the most profound sense—a willingness to lay down one's life for the man beside you in the fight.

In its most profound sense, servant-leadership is what Jesus lived and taught.

Excuse me for hyphenating servant and leadership. I firmly believe the best leaders understand that the *second word* must precede *the first*.

As in *servant-leadership*.

Many Biblical scholars view Mark 10:45 as Jesus' mission statement: "For even Son of Man did not come to be served, but to serve, and to give his life as a ransom for many."

Jesus repeatedly taught about servant-leadership: "The first shall be last . . . "love one another as I have loved you. If anyone would follow me . . .

One of my favorite passages is from Jesus' words in the Gospel of John:

"Greater love has no man than to lay down his life for his friends."

Jesus lived out his teaching on servant-leadership when he willingly laid down his life as a ransom for our sins.

A true servant-leader is never about getting.

It's always about giving.

It's never about looking out for number one.

It's always about serving those around you.

Giving and serving. Probably two of the finest verbs in the English language.

Servant-Leadership.

How do you recognize this type of servant-leadership?

As I said earlier, you'll know it when you see it.

Chapter 40

The Corner Post

"Give me a place to stand, and I'll move the world."

—Archimedes

I stand beside the Corner Post, looking west toward the swamp. I'd better hurry. It's nearly sunset, and there's a lot to do.

The Corner Post isn't any ordinary fence post; It separates the Iles/Wagnon homestead from our neighbors and nearby pine plantations.

It is stout, standing about chest high, the thickness of a small dinner plate. It's *stout.*

That's a good word to describe the Corner Post: I've pushed against it since childhood, and it's never given an inch. It's *stout.*

It's a treasure in our family. It's the solidest thing on this entire homestead. It's a *witness post* at the NE corner of John and Sarah Wagnon's original homestead. They put this post in the ground in the late 19th Century.

It outlasted them, and seven generations later, it's just as stable as ever.

Stable. I like that word. *Stability.* The world needs a lot more stability. The Corner Post will outlast me and probably generations to come. It's that stable and steadfast.

Standing at the Corner Post, I have a clear view of the two houses that have shaped my life—the home I grew up in and the Old House.

Now, the Corner Post isn't pretty. It's gnarled. *Gnarled:* that's one of the most attractive things about the Corner Post: it's gnarled, twisted, fire-blackened, and scarred.

It's withstood the test of time. Because of its resiny heart, it's impervious to rot, weather, and insect damage.

The sun has just set, and twilight descends over the woods.

To get my bearings, I place my compass atop the Corner Post and set it to 270 degrees due west. I'm hunting today, but I don't have a gun. I'm carrying a double-bit ax, compass, and roll of survey flagging.

I'm on the hunt for an old, abandoned fence buried under years of forest debris. Following my compass due west from the Corner Post, I push through the underbrush, hunting for a strand of wire or downed post.

I work my way west toward Crooked Bayou, fighting through a tangled thicket of rotten limbs, chest-head-high briar patches, and downed trees.Our land has never recovered from a series of hurricanes and ice storms that devastated our once-open woods, and it will never look the same.

* * *

I trip over something, kick at it, and dislodge a weathered, blackened fence post. I heft it up; it's heavy.

Laying the post on the ground, I split it with my ax, revealing the rich yellow heart. Then, I breathed in the unforgettable smell of pine sap.

My daddy always said that if you could make a cologne that smelled like pine sap, every man in Beauregard Parish would buy it.

I'd buy a bottle for sure.

I have just uncovered a treasure trove: a rich-lighter fencepost, perfect kindling for starting fires.

Now, I'm on the trail. I grasp a loose strand of rusty barbed wire in the under-brush and follow it to the next post.

I begin working my way toward Crooked Bayou, marking the fence line with surveyor's flagging, Every twenty feet or so, I find another fence post. Most are on the ground, but others are standing as upright as they were the day they were put down.

I push on an upright post. It stubbornly resists my efforts to twist or dislodge it. It won't break off; I've got to pull it up. The exposed part of the fence posts have been weathered, burned, and scarred, but the posts below ground are thicker and set. That's why they're so difficult to dislodge.

I strike it with the flat side of my ax, stinging my hands as it bounces off with a clang.

I step back. This pine post seems to say: *Bud, I've been here a lot longer than you, and I'm not going to give up without a fight.*

I tilt it back and forth until I've wallowed a hole and can now pull it out of the ground. As I heft each one, I find that they are still heavy due to the rich heart sap that has prevented rot for well over a century.

Post by post, I work my way west, tossing the posts out of the thicket into the neighbor's pasture.

Then I happened upon a hefty post I immediately named the "Beast." Although it's not quite the size of my Corner Post, it's probably a first-cousin-once-removed. It won't budge. It'll take several men, a shovel, and some cussing to get this big boy out.

It's probably several feet deep and, like most pine posts, thicker at the bottom. We may have to get my dentist, Dr. Greg Robinson, to extract the Beast.

Whoever succeeds in besting the Beast will have ample pine kindling to get them through the entire winter.

Then, maybe they'll skip the Beast and leave it alone as a hidden treasure.

Walking past it, I find a long line of rich-lighter posts hidden in the underbrush.

I have plenty of posts for my fireplace. There's no need to be greedy.

I shoulder my ax. "I'll see you boys later."

* * *

Sitting on the truck's tailgate, I think about the life history story of the Beast and its smaller sibling posts.

Family lore is that this fence line was built about one hundred and twenty years ago. When its longleaf mother fell, a part of the rich rot-free *heart* became the Beast.

Mature longleaf pines typically reach an age of 100-150 years old.

If my math is correct, it's not a stretch to state that the Beast came from a nearby longleaf that had grown since the mid-18th Century.

That was before the American Revolution ended in 1783, when the French and Spanish contested this land, which they would call the Neutral Territory, and before the first Europeans made a footprint on what is now *"our family land."*

When that pine seedling sprouted from a cone seed, this land was still the domain of the First American peoples. The Beast has a history stretching back that far, maybe beyond.

As I load the other fenceposts in the truck, I'm in awe of what I'm holding in my hand, how small I am, and how brief life is.

Twilight is fading toward dusk. The swamp seems deeper and spookier at this time of evening. As I boy, I pick up my pace coming out at dusk. There's no telling what might be lurking behind the next beech tree.

The first stars are now appearing through the trees.

Before getting in my truck, I take my cell phone from my pocket to text my son Clint.

He and his wife Amanda recently built a beautiful country home in Rapides Parish, on the edge of Kisatchie National Forest.

It has an indoor and outdoor fireplace.

I text Clint:

Clint, I have your house-warming present.

I've found a long line supply of rich-lighter fence posts hidden in Crooked Bayou Swamp.

I'm giving it to you as part of your inheritance. A warning is in order: you'll have to get past the Beast to get them.

However, you, Amanda, Jack, Sydney, and Ellen, must meet me there to claim your endowment.

Love,

Daddy

I think of how Clint's grandchildren might sit by a warm fire kindled by one of these fenceposts—from a line of pine posts *planted* by their descendants.

As I leave the woods, dusk is fading into nightfall, and I drive through the pasture toward the welcoming lights of my mom's house.

I unload the fence posts in a pile. Before leaving, I walk over to pay my respects to the Corner Post.

I rest my hand against it.

It's strong.

It's stable.

It's solid.

It's built to last.

I'm reminded that while the world seems to be shaking on its very foundations, here at the old Corner Post, things are as stable and steadfast as ever.

I hum a line of a favorite hymn,

"On Christ the solid rock I stand,

All other ground is sinking sand,

All other ground is sinking sand."

Chapter 41

Roy and Loki

I 'm on the sidewalk outside Tamp and Grind Coffee, waiting for our weekly homeless Bible study to begin.

That's when I saw Roy. His face was a mask of pain, and his puffy eyes were ample testimony he'd been crying. Roy's countenance and body language revealed deep physical pain. It's hard to hide.

Grief. Roy was grieving.

I looked for Loki, Roy's dog and constant companion. It was clear something had happened to Loki.

Many homeless people have dogs, and they are much more than pets. They comfort their owners during their hopeless wanderings.

I had observed Roy and Loki weekly at Church on the Levee. While Loki sat tethered, his master tenderly stroked his back throughout the entire service. Clearly, this black and tan hound helped calm Roy's demons.

But today, Loki was missing, and Roy was obviously in deep pain. Someone whispered. "Loki was killed. Someone shot him."

I was shocked. Loki was a gentle dog always tied to Roy by a red leash. The story was murky: when you live on the street, many things can happen, most of them bad.

I walked over to Roy. I also know the deep pain of losing a beloved dog. I put my arm around his shoulder. "I'm so sorry, Roy. I know how much Loki meant to you. I'm truly sorry for your loss." I've learned that fewer words and more physical touch are needed in the face of grief.

As Bible study began, I took my seat in a wrought iron outdoor chair. My dog, Bandit, was under my feet, leashed to a chair leg.

Bandit is my constant companion and great company. He's a mutt from the animal shelter. We have a mutual admiration society. I saved him from the pound and an uncertain future. He faithfully sat beside me during the darkest depths of a depression that shook my life to its foundation.

We are grateful for each other, and that's why we enjoy each other's company. That's why he's with me today. I simply enjoy being with him.

Roy takes a chair beside me, his head in his hands. I can sense the sorrow flowing from his soul.

Evidently, Bandit recognizes it, too. He rises and walks over, placing his muzzle on Roy's shoe. He eventually put his paws on Roy's knees, and Roy began stroking his back.

Bandit was vigilant in his duty post throughout the entire study.

I looked up at several of my friends. They nodded with knowing smiles.

The Bible study ended.

Roy shuffled away.

One of our leaders, Anna Marie, nodded at Bandit. "That dog's a comfort dog. He knew just what to do. He knew Roy needed his presence."

I silently nodded. *I don't believe animals have souls, but I do sense God has put a spark of something inside a dog that can sense when a person is hurting.*

We don't call them man's best friend for nothing.

Chapter 42

The Baygall

I learned to hunt in Crooked Bayou Swamp. Our family land extended to the west and across the Bayou to where I reached timber company land. Daddy taught me the areas where the squirrel population was highest. He sketched crude maps pointing out landmarks and streams on our land.

Past our landline, Daddy circled a grove of trees on his map. "That's where the bay gall is."

When I was young, Daddy took me to the Baygall. I believed he and I were the only Iles men who knew its location, and I believed no one else in our family had wandered this far.

Invariably, I was drawn to this unique stand of trees, surrounded by wide-open fields of tall grass in every direction.

Because it was such a special place on my hunting excursions, I gave it a *proper* name: The Baygall.

I became *my* Baygall.

You're probably saying, "What is a baygall?"

If you live in Alexandria, you probably drive by a large one weekly.

More on that later.

The National Park Service defines "A 'bay gall' as an area in the woods *where water collects at the bottom of a poorly drained depression. Debris from surrounding vegetation steeps into the water, causing it to lose oxygen and become acidic.*

Baygalls are named for the woody plants of sweet bay and *gall*berry ho*lly, which are commonly found around these areas.*

In Europe, a baygall is often called a copse, which is defined as a small stand of trees. Winnie the Pooh lived in a baygall called the 100-Acre Wood. He called it a spinney, a small *wood* with undergrowth.

Wood or woods? In a *wood*, you count the trees (eventually) because they have clear borders.

That's not true in the *woods*.

Some definitions call a baygall a "thicket," but My Baygall was clear of any briars or small bushes. It was open, and populated with a tall cathedral of trees: water oaks, pin oaks, and hickory.

My boyhood hunting years were before four-wheelers, posted signs, and hunting leases. The only easily accessible way to the Baygall was through our land and across Crooked Bayou.

I'd walk through it, shotgun on my shoulder. I wasn't really hunting as much as roaming. To my thirteen-year-old mind, the baygall had a sinister feel to it. It was much darker and foreboding than the open grasslands surrounding it.

There was a faint trail through it, and it was always wet. If in tennis shoes, the common squirrel hunting footwear of my youth, they and my socks were soon soaked.

When I first read *Tolkien's The Hobbit* as a young teenager, I shuddered when Bilbo and his band of dwarves entered the dreaded Dark Woods.

I'd been there. I knew Bilbo and Frodo's dark woods were an enormous baygall.

The year I returned from college and found the Baygall razed, drained, and planted in pines was a day of profound sadness.

I had lost a secret friend.

My Baygall was gone.

A timber company may have owned it, but it had belonged to me.

There's a baygall still standing in Alexandria. Many of you pass it . . .

. . . or circle it daily.

It's called the Alexandria Traffic Circle. The swamp inside the circle is a large baygall.

Over the years, I've peered into its thick woods and swampy palmetto cover, wondering what was in there.

That's when a plan formed in my mind, but first, you need to know about the notorious roadway that circles the baygall.

It's called the Alexandria Traffic Circle.

No one likes it.

Everyone seems to hate it.

Due to its four entrance/exit lanes, it is the site of many fender benders.

There was an oft-repeated story about Alexandria and Pineville prior to Interstate 49:

"The reason that North and South Louisiana are so different and disconnected is that you can't get from north to south because of the Traffic Circle in Alexandria."

* * *

I've never heard anyone say anything good about the Alexandria Traffic Circle. It's a huge oval monstrosity that makes a nearly one-mile circle. Four major highways lead onto/off the circle.

What makes it such an obstacle is there are two counterclockwise lanes, and if you're not in the outer lane, you will "circle the circle" endlessly as other drivers peel off and others zoom into any opening.

Conversely, if a traveler takes the wrong exit and stops for directions, they are invariably told, "Well, you go back to the Circle and . . ."

The correct name for a traffic circle is a roundabout. Several smaller roundabouts in Alexandria seem to work fine.

I learned a great deal about roundabouts living in Africa. You've never driven until you weave through a clogged roundabout in Kampala, Uganda. You're driving on the wrong side of the road, and it quickly becomes apparent that there are no rules on yielding. It's every man, or motorcycle, for himself.

Back here in Alexandria, sometimes when DeDe and I go out for our Friday night date, just for fun, I'll make several orbits around the Traffic Circle. "The extra mileage makes it feel like a real date."

However, the South Circle lives on in infamy and confusion. It's the site of collisions on a weekly, if not daily, basis. It's very common to see a police unit and two drivers outside their dented vehicles on the shoulder of the circle.

I've read accounts that traffic circles and roundabouts prevent wrecks, but you'd be hard-pressed to find a true believer in Alex (as the locals call Alexandria).

It's no coincidence that a local personal injury lawyer built a three-story office on the circle. The story is that he has a commanding view of the chaos in the circle. Word is that he's thinking of installing a drive-thru.

The swampy land *inside* the traffic circle is a *baygall*.

This thick grove of trees is a source of mystery. It's a swampy area full of palmetto and standing water.

One winter, I decided to wade across the Traffic Circle Baygall. I carefully chose cold weather to avoid snakes and possible gator encounters. I carried a stick to probe for stump holes as I carefully squished my way into the baygall.

The water was about knee-deep, and the swamp was murky and forbidding as I climbed over fallen trees and swished aside the thick palmetto fronds.

The sun had set, and it was already twilight inside the bay. The city lights were obscured, and the traffic noise was muffled.

I patted my trusty flashlight in my back pocket.

It was more like being in the Atchafalaya Swamp instead of the busiest section of a city.

I scared up two wood ducks in a small open area of the swamp. I wondered if it was legal to shoot ducks in the city limits. It didn't matter. I wouldn't have shot these ducks anyway.

At dusk, I waded out of the Circle swamp, returning to civilization.

As I walked around the circle back to my truck, I was reminded of the oddity that the South Traffic Circle is both legendary and notorious.

From time to time, *The Town Talk* does an article about plans to replace the South Traffic Circle with a series of overpasses and ramps that would span the baygall.

Like most Cenla residents, I'll believe it when I see it.

Unlike my Dry Creek Baygall in Dry Creek, I believe Alexandria's baygall will stand the test of time much beyond my life.

Chapter 43

I Am My Brother's Keeper

I never met David Colvin Manning, but I wished I had. I know I would have liked him. He seemed that kind of man.

I read his obituary in my Sunday copy of *The Town Talk*. I'm one of the few people who still read a paper newspaper. There's something about the feel of newsprint in your hands.

Out of habit, I always read the obituaries. Sadly, good obituaries have gone out of style. Many times, the finest writing I've seen in a newspaper was a written obituary.

The same seemed true about David Colvin Manning's obituary. Reading it, I knew I was poorer because we never met for a hot cup of Community.

Here's part of his obituary:

"David was a lineman for thirty years and then worked for T and D Solutions, a utility service company, as a foreman for distribution, retiring in 2016.

"He was a crew leader who was loved and respected by those who worked for him and with him. He was known as a hard worker who prioritized fairness and the safety of his men.

"He was A Brother's Keeper."

That final short sentence caught my attention. *He was a Brother's Keeper.*

When I first moved to Alexandria, I sat next to a group of workers for T and D Construction.

I've always been curious. Sometimes, this gets me in trouble, but most of the time, I've learned a great deal and made new friends.

"Men, I don't mean to interrupt your meal, but why do you wear the patch on your sleeve: I am my Brother's Keeper?"

One of the men said, "You see, we work in high-line construction. This means we are high in the air and close contact with high-voltage lines. We must take care of each other, looking out for the safety of the entire group, especially the men up in the air.

"When you're working up high, you're truly at the mercy of those on the ground. They literally hold your life in their hands.

"When we say we are our Brother's Keeper, it's a solemn promise to take care of each other."

That left a deep impression on me.

That's why when I saw David Colvin Manning's obituary, I knew all I needed to know about the man. He was a Brother's Keeper.

Loved and respected.

Worked for and with him.

A hard worker with fairness.

Fair with the safety of his men as his first consideration.

And *He was a Brother's Keeper.*

May it be said of us all.

Chapter 44

A Dry Creek Conspiracy

I'm a conspiracy theorist. Miriam-Webster calls a conspiracy "The secret act of conspiring together."

I'm not sure whose idea it was. The conspiracy just happened.

Eleanor Andrews was my fifth-grade teacher. We had a mutual admiration that existed from the time I was ten until she died in 2000.

In the years leading up to her death, Eleanor Andrews was the victim of a conspiracy.

A Dry Creek conspiracy.

A conspiracy of love.

* * *

I don't recall any meeting or committee to flesh it out. Dry Creek just did it.

In the latter season of her life, Eleanor Andrews was homebound. She was a widow-woman. She'd lost her husband, Red, years ago and lived as a widow longer than she'd been married.

She was what the old timers called a "widder-woman," as in a widow-woman.

If they were homebound, they were called "shut-ins," as in, "The deacons will be visiting with all of the shut-ins this week."

My great-great-great-grandmother lost her husband, John Wesley Wagnon, in the Civil War in 1863.

Nancy Wagnon lived in Dry Creek as a war widow until her death in 1912. I know enough about the Dry Creek Community to know that her family and neighbors took care of her for nearly a half-century.

Widow-woman; Shut-in; Homebound.

These aren't derogatory terms. Being a shut-in or homebound means you're unable to leave home without help to do the things we all take for granted.

A shut-in is dependent on others; in our culture, that is best done by family. But none of Mrs. Eleanor's three sons lived in Dry Creek.

Eleanor Andrews had a deep fear: a fear of spending the last part of her life in the sterile environment of a nursing home in DeRidder.

And that's when the conspiracy began.

As the years passed, neighbors pitched in. In a small community like Dry Creek, a neighbor is much more than proximity. Because Eleanor Andrews had taught two generations of Dry Creek children, her neighborly circle stretched pretty far.

Of course, her church pitched in. The Bible talks about taking care of widows and orphans, and that's what her church did. A caring church will gather around and support its members in times of illness, grief, and trouble.

I've often wondered, "What do people without a church home do when a crisis comes?"

Neighbors began cleaning, shopping, taking care of her beloved yard and flowers, bringing her meals, and driving her to doctor's appointments.

Everyone pitched in and did their part, and it wasn't difficult— It was a privilege.

Mrs. Eleanor died at age eighty-two. She spent her last few days in a hospital, but she never saw the inside of a nursing home.

Thanks to a conspiracy of love. A conspiracy of kindness.

A Dry Creek conspiracy.

Chapter 45

Screen Door Living

S ince we moved out of the Old House in 1960, I've never lived in a house with actual screen doors. I'm talking about a wooden screen door: the lower half is covered in hardware cloth, and the spring hinges have a strong inside hook latch.

The kind of door that went *whap* when you let go of it.

Here's what I know about screen doors: the Old House has eleven exterior doors, nine of which have working screen doors.

I asked my elders, and no one could remember the exterior doors ever being locked. The keyhole locks were unused and useless, and no one had a key.

Eleven outside doors. Nine screen doors.

I've always had a love affair with screen doors. I still walk through the Old House, opening screen doors, to hear them flap.

How do you describe the sound of a screen door slamming?

Wham.

Flap.

Bam.

Creak.

Whack.

It's hard to describe the sound because each of the nine-screen doors at the Old House has its own personality and timbre.

Some of you may have never heard an old-time wooden screen door slam. All I can tell you is when you hear one, you'll remember it.

It was one of the sweetest sounds of my childhood, as four generations of ancestors opened and shut the doors all day long.

At the Old House, there are varying degrees of slamming. There are a few slam trackers that will literally hit you in the butt if you don't get out of the way. I call them Mousetraps, as in, "Don't let the screen door hit you on your way out."

Among the nine-screen doors at the Old House, there are several lazy boys. Their hinge springs are worn and loose. They yawn as they leisurely close, making only a slight tap on the door jamb.

The Old House had no central heating/cooling (it still doesn't), so keeping the screen doors latched was necessary due to mosquitoes and other insects. It sits on the edge of Crooked Bayou Swamp, so keeping insects out was a priority. Most of the screen doors stayed latched.

If you wanted a chewing out, leave a screen ajar. It was the cardinal sin of mosquito control.

"Shut that door behind you."

The latches were simple hook and eye. They weren't always easy to latch due to misalignments of the screen, door, and door jamb. Because the screens were often latched, as a boy, I often made wide circles around the porches, pulling on screen doors.

The screen doors were particularly challenging at night. The older folks, being early risers, were "latched and lights out."

Every screen was secure. A few could be opened with a pocketknife, but you risked damaging the latch or door jamb. You'd have to make noise to awaken someone. You'd call out softly, hoping someone would hear you above the window fan.

You can rattle the door, but that will awaken half the house. A shaken screen door makes a really irritating sound, and whoever gets out of bed to unlatch it will be irritable, too.

So, you wanted one screen door unlatched.

My MaMa Pearl, who loved me with all of her heart, would leave the middle room door unlatched so I could slip in undetected.

"Baby, is that you?"

"It's me, MaMa. Thanks."

"Goodnight, Baby."

Chapter 46

Silence and Solitude

"There is no 'quiet place' in the white man's cities. There is no place to hear the unfurling of leaves in spring or the rustle of insect's wings. But perhaps it is because I am a savage and do not understand."

—Chief Seattle

1854

I've been musing on silence and solitude and how they relate to our spiritual lives.

Silence is a state with no distractions.

Solitude is simply being alone in that quiet silence.

Silence precedes it; Solitude always follows silence.

It's challenging to have a spirit of solitude without being surrounded by silence. We don't like being alone. We're scared of silence, just like a child in the dark.

You cannot have solitude without silence.

Silence is the art of being quiet.

Solitude in a place in the heart.

These are not passive words. We're going to work hard to capture silence and solitude. They're elusive in the 21st Century, but it's worth it.

Then, we must remove distractions during our time of silence and solitude. We live in a world of distractions, many of them self-created.

Can I be honest? I struggle with creating solitude and silence in my life—I'm still learning and then re-learning.

I'm no expert. I'm a fellow learner.

A fellow struggler.

* * *

Spiritually, silence and solitude should lead us to a quiet time with God.

Time alone with God.

A quiet time.

Quiet time: It's often called a QT.

A QT can be anywhere.

It can be anytime.

QTs can often be measured in blocks of time, which can vary from minutes to days or beyond.

An effective quiet time will include Bible study, prayer, and meditation.

Meditation is simply silent thoughtfulness about God. It means listening for God's still, small, powerful voice.

Silence, solitude, and listening must be free of distractions.

My greatest distractions are my screens. That is why I place a beach towel over my work desk, papers, and laptop after the evening meal.

I tell them good night and promise to see them tomorrow morning. This allows me to take a well-needed non-guilty break until the next morning.

I don't do as well on this habit: sometimes, later in the evening, I place my precious iPhone into an empty shoebox.

I'm still working on that one.

The key is to eliminate distractions so I can focus on things that *really* matter: my wife, spiritual solitude thoughts, and a time of relaxation.

It works for me. Come up with your own plan.

In closing, here is my favorite quiet-time story:

T.W. Hunt, the author of *The Mind of Christ,* shared the following at Dry Creek Baptist Camp:

"One morning, I'd not felt as close to the Lord as I wished, so I did something strange: I poured a second cup of coffee and took it with me to my back porch.

"Setting the second cup down, I said, 'Lord, I want to invite you to have a cup of coffee with me. This morning—today—I want more than anything to visit with you.'"

Dr. Hunt smiled as he finished his story: "God was already there. I just needed a visible reminder."

I've shared Dr. Hunt's story over the years, and it always elicits smiles and nods.

I love asking folks where they go for their quiet time with God. It is often a room, a specific chair, a bathroom, a patio, or an outdoor place of solitude.

It might even be where you place two steaming cups of coffee.

Chapter 47

The Journaling Life

"I worship when I write, and I write when I worship."

I haven't always been an author, but I've always been a writer.

There's a difference.

Writing. It's what I do.

It's also who I am.

If I never published another book, I'd still write. Writing has always been a big part of my life.

I write something every day. *A writer is someone who wrote today.*

My journals are where I write down my dreams. It's where I *vocalize* my goals.

You don't need a leather-bound line journal. I've journaled on everything, most of it cheap.

I'm currently using a small journal entitled "Field Notes."

Field Notes. Field notes are the process of observing and taking note of things, usually involving recording these insights in a book. They are a method of chronicling events and places.

Field notes. I've always liked that term. My dad was a land surveyor, and he carried a pocket-sized field notebook. He kept sketches, notes, and charts in his book.

My field notes journal is similar to Daddy's. It's full of the markings of life, sketches, maps, web addresses, and my list of the things I hope to accomplish today.

If you saw a page in my journal, you'd say, "What can you get out of the tangled bird's nest of erasures and highlights?

That's why I journal in pencil. Using an eraser isn't a cardinal sin, especially for a writer.

Erasures are permitted in writing and life.

Don't put "Final Draft" on anything you write.

Writing, like life, is always a work in progress.

* * *

Write it down!
"The faintest pencil is better than the sharpest mind."

* * *

There is power in vocalizing your dreams, hopes, and goals.

Shout them from the housetop, but don't forget to write them down.

Once you write them down on paper, they become yours. They become visible—maybe only to you—but visible nonetheless.

My journals are where I scribble my dreams and aspirations.

Looking back over the pages of countless journals, I read of dreams that never happened.

That's okay. Those unfulfilled dreams still made me a better person by bravely putting them on paper. Many of my written dreams haven't come true, but many have because I took the step of writing them down.

I firmly believe many of the accomplishments of my life began with a sentence in a long-ago shelved journal.

The Three Questions

After a quarter of a century of being published, I still get these same three questions.

Routinely, some old fart will walk up,

"I bet half of those stories aren't true. You're just making them up, aren't you?"

I'm not guilty of making up my stories, but I take full responsibility for embellishing them. That's what good storytellers do. They tell a good story and make it even better.

I grew up in that culture of storytelling. Hundreds of faces flicker across, and I recall the masters of storytelling I grew up around.

Another question I get repeatedly is, "Where do you come up with all of those stories?"

I tried all kinds of replies: the wind in the pines, an owl calling my name, and voices from my ancestors.

But it all comes down to this: I tell stories from the heart; from my heart to your heart.

Those stories make me laugh, wince, shake my head and cry.

Throughout *Where I Come From,* I've quoted, "No tears in the writer, no tears in the reader." I've learned that if a story moves me to laughter or tears, it will probably do the same for others.

For some reason, this fourteenth book has been the most emotional one I've written. It seems the tears are ready to leak out as I read a chapter or hear a new story, and I'm pleased.

It may be my age. I hope my heart grows more tender as the years pass. I hope you sense that in the pages of *Where I Come From.*

I believe the real reason for my current emotional state is that I'm mentally healthy again. Many of you know that I struggle with depression. I've been through some dark valleys over the previous years; some that I wasn't sure I'd crawl out of.

There are so many symptoms of clinical depression, but two of the most painful ones in my journey *through* depression are a loss of creativity coupled with a dry soul that sheds no tears.

I'm grateful to God for having those creative juices and tears back, so if some of the ink on your copy is tear-stained, please understand. It just means I'm writing from a full heart.

The final question I am asked is, "Do you think you'll ever run out of stories?"

"Heck no. I had to cull some really good stories for this book. There's plenty more where these come from. Hopefully, you'll see them in future books.

I'm in a season where I'm confident I'm doing God's will and work. In my various careers, I've always had that peace of purpose, and I definitely have it now.

So, for this season, as long as God allows, I'm going to open my journal, pick up my pencil, and write.

I'm going to write stories.

* * *

I've always been a writer, and I've kept a lifetime of journals. However, much of what I've written will never see the light of day. That's all right. Just consistently putting words on paper has made me a better, stronger person.

There's something magical when you put a pen to paper.

It's been a habit ingrained in me from childhood. I remember the first written prose I ever wrote. On a sheet of lined notebook paper, I scratched,

By thunder,

This world is a wonder.

I showed it to my mother. She gushed about the creative imagination I had. Of course, Momma would've have bragged if I'd written a crooked line down the sheet.

I proudly tacked up my work on art for the world to see.

A few years older, I cringed at the pitiful seven words on two lines of lined notebook paper. I crumpled it and threw it in the waste basket.

However, I've come to realize there is a great truth there: *this world is a wonder*!

In, fact those seven words sum up a life of observation and writing— fourteen books and a lifetime of journals— An amazement at the world around me and my attempt to put it on paper.

I'd put it this way: *By thunder, this world is a wonder!*

* * *

You don't have to be an author to be a writer.

You may prefer to write what will never see the light of day,

Long after I've authored my last book, I'll still be scratching out ideas, outlines, drafts, and sketching in the latest in an endless line of journals over half a century.

I journal.

That makes me a writer. A writer is someone who wrote today.

I write because I'm a storyteller. I come from a culture of Southern rural piney-woods storytellers.

I've found it's the best way to get a point across or entertain.

Tell a story. You can't go wrong. That's what *Where I Come From* is. It's a book of stories about the people and places I love.

* * *

"If there's a book that you want to read, but it hasn't been written yet,

then you must write it."

-Toni Morrison

Not everyone will write a book, but everyone has a book inside them.

It's your choice whether to turn it loose on the world.

If you don't write that book, who will? As in, "I'm the only person who can write that book. I'd better get busy."

I've written my last book query letter, which is a begging letter sent to editors and agents asking for their blessing and publication.

That means I'll never receive another rejection letter. Like every long-term author, I've got a stack of rejections that would choke a full-grown golden retriever.

I've thrown them away.

We're living in a new publishing world where every author can produce a great-looking book at an economical cost. It's called Indie publishing.

They call it self-publishing or print-on-demand (P.O.D.). The best pathway to publishing your book is with KDP: Kindle Direct Publishing.

If you've got that book in you that's screaming to get out, go for it. There's never been a better time to become an author.

Jump off the cliff.

Cross the Rubicon.

Toss your hat over the wall.

Above all, write.

Remember, a writer is someone who wrote today.

"It is a wonder that God uses squiggles on a page to do His work in the hearts and minds of people."

-Celebration of Discipline

Richard Foster

Chapter 48

Pine Kindling

"I'm not certain about the eight wonders of the World, but I'm sure one of them is rich, lighter pine kindling."

I have a startling confession to make: I'm going to Ace Hardware this afternoon to buy some pine kindling.

I'm glad my ancestors didn't live long enough to see a Dry Creek man pay good money for rich, lighter kindling. We recently moved into a house in Alexandria with a fireplace. I've been waiting for the October cool spells that mean logs on the fire and the sweet smells of burning wood and rich pine resin. It makes me think of home.

Here's why I'm ashamed of buying rich-lighter at a hardware store:

The Louisiana Pineywoods of my youth were covered in an abundance of stumps and heart pine from the cutover of the virgin longleafs. But those days are gone. Seldom will you find rich-lighter in the woods. Recently, I walked most of my family's land and did not find one stick, knot, fencepost, or stump of rich lighter. I was saddened that an era had passed.

There's another reason I'm sad. When DeDe and I moved to Dry Creek, we had the largest pine knot pile in the community. We'd inherited' this *lifetime* supply of pine kindling when we bought our house.

Until it burned up.

Here's the sad story: I was burning in the back field when suddenly, the February wind picked up and turned out of the South. Instantly, a small brush fire became a raging monster.

The flames spread rapidly through the dead knee-high grass—as fast as I could, I ran ahead with a wet grass sack. But no one person, nor any wet sack, was going to stop this fire.

DeDe and the boys came running out of the house. Armed with brooms, buckets, and a shovel, we battled the fire until the heat drove us back.

We stood together as the fire engulfed my tall pine knot pile. As soon as the brush fire reached the pine pile, it was completely engulfed in flames. We watched helplessly as my "lifetime supply" of pine knots literally went up in smoke.

In fifteen minutes, it was over. A smoking pile of ashes was left where my pine knot pile had towered.

One of the boys said, "Well, Daddy, it was an impressive fire."

Another one added, "That sure was some kind of black smoke."

I'd burned up my pine pile.

* * *

I think of my pine knot pile when I read Jesus' words in Matthew 6.

He reminds us that all earthly treasures will someday rust, corrode, rot, or—as in my case—burn up.

Jesus told us to hoard heavenly treasures – the things that really last: eternal things.

The only things I've seen that really last are God's word, His love, and people's souls. Therefore, that's where our treasures should be.

Earthly treasures have their place, but we should never forget they are only temporary. Like my pine knot pile, earthly treasures can leave us quickly and unexpectedly.

However, the things of God are the only things that really matter, and they last forever.

As the Robert Duvall character in the movie, "Broken Trails" said,

"It's always wrong to measure a man's wealth by how much money he has."

So, pine knot piles, IRAs, jewels, titles, land, and fame aren't the measure of wealth and success.

Indeed, "The things that *really* matter aren't things."

Jesus said it clearly in Matthew 6:19-21:

"Do not store up for yourselves treasures on earth, where moth and rust destroy, and where thieves break in and steal.

But store up for yourselves treasures in heaven, where moth and rust do not destroy, and where thieves do not break in and steal. For where your treasure is, your heart will also be there."

Postscript

A giving man named Don.

"Can you meet me at Tractor Supply? I've got something for you."

It was my friend Don Gray. I had no idea what he had for me.

A word in edgewise: Don Gray will be upset about being outed in this story; he prefers to *give under the radar.* He loves to give—he's left a lifetime of giving to the East Beauregard community, especially young people.

Don is a big, gruff-talking lifetime logger. But don't be fooled—behind that exterior beats the heart of a kind and compassionate man.

When we met at Tractor Supply, he had two feed sacks full of rich lighter.

"I heard you lost your pine knot pile and can't find any in Alexandria, and I thought you might use this."

I thanked him profusely until he got in his truck and roared away.

Standing there, the thought hit me: there are gifts, and there are *Gifts.*

The latter come from the heart and meet a need. These types of gifts require foresight, planning, some work, and a double dose of kindness.

Don Gray's two sacks of lighter pine took me through the winter. Each time I split a piece, I was reminded that the best gifts always come from the heart.

Especially gifts like rich-lighter pine.

* * *

"The only gift is a portion of thyself."

—Ralph Waldo Emerson

Chapter 49

Spears Cemetery

I was born in a small town

And I can breathe in a small town.

Gonna die in a small town,

That's probably where they'll bury me.

—John Mellencamp, "Small Town"

The Little Girl

I drive through the fog of an October morning on my way to Dry Creek Cemetery. My wipers fight a losing battle with the Louisiana fog and humidity. Parking my truck, I peer through the mist for the landmark of our cemetery: a lone old red cedar. I always think of the Little Girl buried beneath it.

There are various versions of the little girl and her first burial in Spears Cemetery. One of my mentors, Mr. Leonard Spears, shared this version with me on the origins of our cemetery and the Little Girl's grave.

Dry Creek Cemetery, originally called Spears Cemetery, began about twenty years after the Civil War ended. A family was traveling through Dry Creek bound for Texas, and a small daughter died while camped there.

Mr. Leonard Spears' grandfather, Len Spears, offered to bury the child in the corner of his field. Because no permanent headstone was available, a wooden marker was placed.

A cedar sapling was planted by the Little Girl's grave. Over time, her name was forgotten, and her simple wooden marker was displaced, but the small cedar grew.

The Spears clan began burying their dead around the cedar and the grave of the Little Girl. Soon, the spot became known as Spears Cemetery. Families throughout greater Dry Creek began burying their dead there. During the 20th Century, Spears Cemetery became Dry Creek Cemetery. My people are buried there, and I have my own spot picked out.

Many changes have taken place as the cemetery has grown and expanded, but the red cedar, gnarled by storms and weather, still stands, marking the spot where the Little Girl is buried.

The grave of this pioneer child became the first of many in what was originally known as Spears Cemetery. It soon became the primary burial spot in our community. It is a special and sacred place for those who have buried the bodies of loved ones here.

I've always imagined that grieving mother taking one last look from the wagon at the fresh-heaped grave of her daughter. No matter where this family was headed, she probably wondered over the years if anyone even remembered.

Mother, we remember. This story is a testament to the promise the Spears family and Dry Creek community made to you.

We still remember.

No one knew her name, but she'll always be the Little Girl buried under the cedar tree.

The Little Boy

Walking away from the old cedar, my heart is transported back to Africa, and I'm standing in the midst of a refugee camp in dusty, barren northern Uganda.

It was a day I will remember for the rest of my life. Thousands of South Sudanese were fleeing across the Ugandan border due to a senseless civil war. These refugees had lost everything: homes, cattle, land, and were literally at the mercy of the world.

I was with my missionary friend Jay as we walked through the sprawling refugee camp. A Ugandan friend approached, "A child has died. They want you to come help bury the boy."

Jay and I looked at each other. *What would we say?* On the short, bumpy ride through the camp, we discussed this. *What could two Mzungu do to help bury a child in the midst of this chaos?*

As soon as we drove up, I heard the wailing.

It was a wail of chilling, harrowing sorrow that cannot be reproduced under ordinary circumstances. Thirty keening women stood around a small open grave as several women carried a shroud-covered small body and carefully laid it inside an open grave.

There were no men present. They were either dead, fighting in South Sudan, or had stayed behind trying to protect their cattle herd and homes.

The wailing of the women continued. It was the sound of pure grief that came from deep within the women as if a torrent of sorrow was pouring out of their souls.

Knowing the transient life of a refugee camp, I wondered how many of the women actually knew the mother and her dead son. I realized that it didn't matter. All of them had suffered similar losses. You don't have to know someone well to grieve with them.

Because of the emaciated state of most refugees, it wasn't easy knowing the age of the white-shrouded body. There's only one thing I learned: he was too young to die. Oddly, we never learned the cause of death of the boy. There are so many ways to die as a refugee.

The family of the dead boy was on the run from the civil war in South Sudan, headed to another distant refugee camp where their tribal neighbors were. They wouldn't be at this burial spot long before moving on. That only made the burial sadder.

The crowd consisted of women speaking a host of tribal languages. Their facial markings distinguished them as being from rival tribes fighting back in South Sudan.

Today, it didn't seem to matter.

Everyone stared at Jay and me. No one present seemed to speak English until a young woman, who knew a slight bit, stepped forward.

Jay stepped forward and shared from his heart with the assistance of our shaky translator.

I watched the circle of women, realizing that what Jay was saying didn't matter; it was the fact that we were there. We were present at the worst moment of this young mother's life. We showed up and shared her sorrow.

I believe she clearly understood the compassion on Jay's face and the tears in his eyes.

When he finished, the crowd began singing. I didn't know one word, but I felt the inner strength of these brave women, knowing all of them had probably buried a family member somewhere in the past.

The singing stopped, and they lowered the dead child into the grave. The wailing resumed as dirt was shoveled over the shrouded body.

We cried with them. There was nothing else we could do.

There was nothing we should do. We were sent there to be witnesses.

One of the women put a crude cross at the head of the grave.

As Jay and I left, the mother approached us. She took Jay's hands and spoke passionately in her heart language. Our translator said, "She wants to thank you for coming. She cannot believe that two Mzungus would come to help bury her little boy."

I'll never forget that moment.

I can't.

I don't want to forget.

* * *

Strangely, I'd never linked these two stories before. The Little Girl and the Little Boy.

Two women, two mothers, one in North America and the other in Africa, each leaving a gravesite knowing they'll never return.

Worlds apart. From the Nineteenth Century to the Twenty-First Century. Sometimes, those things don't seem to matter.

It's roughly eight thousand miles as the crow flies from the Dry Creek cedar tree to the treeless refugee camp in Northern Uganda, but burying a child must have felt the same regardless of the continent or century.

A little girl buried in the sandy soil of the Louisiana Pineywoods.

A small boy buried in the rich red soil of East Africa.

So far.

Yet so close.

Chapter 50

The Windmill

A merican GIs weren't the only soldiers who showed up in Louisiana during the Second World War.

German POW camps were built throughout Louisiana at our major military bases, Camp Polk, Camp Claiborne, and Camp Livingston. Later, smaller POW satellite camps, like Camp Eunice, opened,

The German POWs worked daily on area farms, filling a void left by the local men who were off fighting in the War.

Most of the POWs had been soldiers in Rommel's Afrika Korp when they were captured in North Africa.

Amazingly, friendships and relationships developed as the young Germans proved themselves dependable and hard-working, laboring alongside the local families.

Despite being the enemy, bonds often developed between the German POWs and farm families.

This is one such story:

Fourth-generation rice farmer Jimmy Loewer shared this story from his home in Mowata, Louisiana.

"During the mid-1960s, a car drove up to our family farm, and a well-dressed middle-aged couple stepped out.

"They were a German couple visiting America. He'd returned to show his wife where he worked as a POW during the War. The man said in passable English, pointing at the windmill. 'I remember the windmill and house. We worked here during the rice harvest that year, and the American couple at this house treated us well. It was 1944, and the wife of the house was pregnant.'"

Jimmy Loewer smiled. "That woman was my mother, and she was pregnant with me."

As I always say, *you cannot make up a story better than the truth.*

* * *

The German POW Graves

I scoffed when I first heard it: Four German POWs buried in the Alexandria National Cemetery. It is located in Pineville, Louisiana, on Shamrock Street. It contains over 10,000 American veteran graves laid out with Arlington-like precision.

There are five German POWs buried among these American graves. I was determined to find them in the eight-acre cemetery. I wandered around until a worker took me to the spot in the southeast corner.

There they were:

Ernst Eggert

Paul Kalks

Willi Kneip

Walter Phelahn

Franz Lohman.

I had a multitude of questions:

Where and *how* did they die?

Why were they buried in an American military cemetery?

Did their families in Germany know their fate?

A historical marker at the cemetery sheds some light: The five POWs were initially interred at Camp Fannin, Texas. At some point, they were moved to Alexandria.

The United States has a longstanding tradition, dating to the Civil War, of proper burial of all soldiers. POWs who died in America were buried "following their national customs." Unless claimed by family or country, their graves remain the responsibility of the United States government to this day.

* * *

I'm determined to delve deeper into this German POW story.

Internet Sleuths: you're invited to dig with me into the story of these five German POWs as well as the history of POW Camps in Louisiana.

If you unearth any clues, contact me at creekbank.stories@gmail.com

Teachers, this sounds like a great school project!

* * *

A Place Called Mowata

"I grew up in a tiny Southern town

I grew up with my family all around."

—Jason Isbell, *Something to Love*

In the earlier story, I shared Jimmy Loewer's fascinating story about the former POW bringing his wife to the Loewer farm in Mowata, Louisiana.

Where is Mowata? It's hard to put your finger on it. Area residents give conflicting views on Mowata's location, as there are no city limits. It is located between the cities of Eunice and Crowley.

Most point to the Mowata Store along La. Hwy 13. For me, the Mowata is to find where the windmill once was on the Loewer farm or the nearby red brick Mowata Baptist Church.

You'll be smack in the middle of downtown Mowata.

Mowata, Louisiana, is a tight-knit German-American Baptist community nestled among the French-speaking Catholic Acadians (or Cajuns) of south Louisiana.

It is an easily overlooked hamlet in the rice belt of Acadia Parish.

There are various stories about how Mowata got its name. The oldest is that a railroad spur passed through the Mowata, and the train would stop along the track for water.

As the steam engine hissed, the engineer would call down,

"*More water. More water.*"

Soon, the stop was known as Mowata, and the name *stuck*.

* * *

One of the reasons I love Mowata is the strong bond with my Pineywoods family.

There are so many similarities with my hometown of Dry Creek, fifty miles away as the crow flies.

Mowata is a community with a proud heritage, tight-knit families, hard-working people working the land, and a deep faith.

That sounds similar to my hometown of Dry Creek. The biggest difference is that they grow rice, and we grow pine trees.

Two of my Iles granddaughters, Emma and Eliza Iles, trace their heritage to Mowata. Their mother, Sara, is half-German-American. Sara's mother, Helen Lingerfelter Knuckles, is a full-blooded German-American with her Mowata roots going back four generations. Helen is from a rice-growing family in the vast Cajun Prairie.

Emma and Eliza Iles straddle two distinct landscapes: the rice fields and the Pineywoods.

Mowata and Dry Creek.

When Sara and Terry Iles married, these two cultures and histories merged.

I hope their two children, Emma and Eliza, will keep one foot each in both Dry Creek and Mowata.

It's more than ironic that these two granddaughters, Emma and Eliza, will live in New Orleans, where Terry teaches Hebrew at New Orleans Baptist Seminary.

New Orleans is definitely different from either Dry Creek or Mowata; there is no comparable place to the Crescent City. I've been privileged to travel much of the world, but I have not seen a city quite like New Orleans.

It's a long way to New Orleans, both literally and figuratively, from Dry Creek and Mowata.

My prayer is those two New Orleans girls will never forget where their people come from.

Chapter 51

The Lost Art of Snake Popping

Most people scoff when I mention it. Few have seen it.

Even fewer believe it.

I've observed it numerous times and t a few times myself, sometimes with success and once or twice with disastrous consequences.

The art of snake popping.

Tinker Mahaffey was the first person I ever saw do it. He jerked a four-foot chicken snake off a sweet gum tree, whirled it around like a lasso, and popped it like a whip.

It wasn't pretty, but it was impressive.

Garrett Greene told me that when he snake-popped a rat snake, his children stood in wild-eyed wonder. "They looked at me as if I was Indiana Jones."

* * *

Of all of the fictional characters I've created in my four novels, Mayo Moore may be my favorite.

Mayo gets center stage in *A Good Place* as he narrates the book in first person.

This is a memorable passage from my second novel, *A Good Place,*

I recently told the following story about Mayo's snake-popping to a senior adult group. An older man on a walker laughed so hard we had to fan him. I'm pretty sure a lady in the second row peed in her pants.

Here it is for you to read, enjoy, and laugh.

Mayo Moore is a young teenager of mixed Irish and Redbone blood. He narrates the entire book, including this rendition of "The Snake-Popping," which takes place in 1860 in Louisiana's No Man's Land, in the area still known as *Ten Mile*.

Here's Mayo Moore:

"About a week later, I learned an important lesson. It resulted in the worst whipping of my life, and it all started with our new corncrib.

Now, my daddy, who'd grown up in snake-less Ireland, was scared to death of snakes—not only poisonous ones—but all snakes. I believe a foot-long garter snake put the same fear of the Lord in him as a huge timber rattler. He loved telling the story of St. Patrick tossing Ireland's snakes off the mountain near his hometown, laughing as he added, "All of the snakes tossed out of Ireland by the Saint landed here in Louisiana."

I didn't inherit that fear of snakes; in fact, I've always been fascinated with them. I grew up in a world where boys caught snakes. Now I wasn't stupid—I was careful with copperheads or cottonmouths, but I wasn't one bit afraid of the harmless ones making up most of our snake population.

I'd learned a great deal about snakes from my Uncle Eli. He was fearless with them and taught me how to identify and handle them. Among his varied talents was one I admired the most: snake-popping.

He'd catch a snake by the tail—most often a chicken snake—and pop the snake like a whip. If snapped with enough force and a tight enough grip on the tail, the snake's head would pop right off.

It was an impressive sight. Eli taught me how to do it, and I was rightfully proud of my newfound skill. On this fateful day, I was cleaning out the corncrib and unearthed a three-foot-long chicken snake under the corn shucks. In spite of its regular diet of rats, which we detested, it had a more enormous appetite for chicken eggs and biddies, so anytime we found one on our place, we killed it. Since it was winter, the snake was sluggish and easily caught.

Just as I left the crib, holding the snake with both hands, was when fate took over. My Irish daddy came around the barn whistling, carrying a pail of milk in his hand.

I thought this was the perfect time to show him my new snake-popping skill, figuring he'd be appropriately impressed with my brave action. Laying the chicken snake on the ground, I grasped its tail and, with a mighty whipping action, propelled the snake in an arc.

And that's when trouble started.

I didn't have as good a grip as I should've, and my whipping motion didn't result in the head popping off—instead, it caused the entire chicken snake to fly out of my hands.

In horror, I watched it fly through the air straight for Daddy, who stood frozen with his mouth open. The snake twirled in a long arc like a stretched rubber band and, on its downward path, landed on Daddy, wrapping itself around his leg.

Momma, who was on the porch and saw it all, later summed it up, 'My man Joe got religion when that snake wrapped around his leg.'

The bucket of milk was the first casualty. It flew through the air, milk spilling in every direction. But that wasn't the end of the flying—Daddy got ahold of the snake and flung it across the yard. Once again, like a thrown rope, the poor snake was airborne, finally hitting the barn wall with a loud thump before sliding to the ground.

I should've sprinted for the safety of the woods, but I could only watch in horror. Daddy was hollering in Irish—which is what he always did when he was mad or scared—and he was a lot of both at the moment. I glanced at the porch for help from Momma, but she stood with her hand over her face, trying to suppress a laughing fit.

I heard her sputter to Daddy, 'Joe, ain't no use cryin' over spilt milk.'

Looking back, I saw my dog Bo charging the helpless snake. Grasping the snake in his mouth, he shook it violently and tossed it through the air—right back toward Daddy.

At least this time, he had time to duck. It cleared his head by about a foot before landing with another "whomp" against the corn crib.

The next movement in this drama did not bode well for me: Daddy was on the move toward me. Collaring me, he began wearing me out with the other. When his hand started hurting, he picked up the empty milk bucket and began walloping me on the behind with it. It didn't hurt, but it sounded like it did. He kept it up a long time, chewing me out with every swing of the bucket. Who knows what he was saying since he was still yelling in Irish.

When he stopped, we both looked to the porch, and Momma was gone. The snake was also gone. It seemed as if its three flights would've dazed or killed it, but evidently, it had cleared the premises. Speaking of clearing out, that's what

I did—going to the woods until Momma called for supper. It was a long time before I tried snake-popping again, and I made sure I was ways from the house."

Postscript

Herb and Becky Cady are our neighbors in Alexandria. They spent twenty years doing mission work among the Maasai tribe in Kenya and Tanzania.

This is Becky's story about a memorable unforgettable day in a Maasai village near the foot of Mt. Kilimanjaro:

"I was teaching a Bible study among a group of Maasai women in a small Tanzanian village near the foot of Mt. Kilimanjaro. The church was typical African bush: thatched roof, mud brick walls, and hard clay floor.

"I was speaking in Swahili, as a local lady translated it into Maasai.

"Suddenly, a large snake slithered in from a crack in the wall. Everyone cowered in fear against the back wall. Africans are fearful of any snake, and this wasn't just any snake. It was a black mamba, the most feared African poisonous snake. In most cases, a black mamba bite is fatal.

"An older Maasai woman stepped forward from the group of ladies, snatched the black mamba by the tail, and swung the snake like a whip before snapping it down with a fierce jerk.

"The snake's head flew off like a shot, thumping against the far wall.

"Holding the headless body aloft in triumph, the woman walked to the door, tossing the headless snake outside with a loud benediction in Maasai,

'In the name of the Lord Jesus, I cast you out of this building.'"

As I often say, you can't make up a story better than that.

Whether it's in Tanzania or Ten Mile.

Chapter 52

Watch Out For the Fish

I t's trendy to put a Christian fish on your car bumper. It is a replica of the simple two-mark symbol used as a secret code by Christians of the first century.

The "Fish-on-the-Car" signals that the person behind the wheel is, hopefully, a Christian. But it is also scary—the responsibility that other drivers around us will watch closely to see if our driving habits model the teachings of Jesus.

I recall the popular bumper sticker of my teen years, "Honk if you love Jesus!"

I heard the story of one happy Christian carload that kept honking at a bumper-stickered Ford 150 in front of them. Their honking brought no reply until the driver put his arm out the window and gave an obscene gesture that was definitely not associated with Jesus.

The same is true with "The Fish." We should be cautious in wearing or exhibiting any symbol representing Christ unless our corresponding actions will bring Him glory, not embarrassment.

I word it this way: *Watch Out for the Fish.*

. . . and that brings me to one of my favorite stories on this subject:

A few summers ago, Clay, my nephew Adam, and I made a hiking trip to the Smoky Mountains of Tennessee. We had a great time walking and enjoying the rugged Appalachian Trail.

After about four days, I sensed the boys had had enough of being in the wild. They'd had enough of the wild side of life. I said, "All right, we'll go home when we see a black bear or it rains."

That night, we had a black bear raid our camp. That's a good story for another time.

Adam said, "Well, Uncle Curt, I guess we can go home now."

We loaded up the following day and headed west on I-20.

Everything went fine until we reached the Alabama-Mississippi state line. As we approached the exit for Toomsuba, Mississippi, the van sounded as if it had run over a landmine. The engine had no power, so we coasted off the interstate into the parking lot of a convenience store.

A quick inspection revealed that our drive shaft was gone. I went into the store and asked the one clerk behind the counter, "How could I get help on car repair?"

He studied me. "Well, Bunyard's Transmission is down the road. Let me give them a call."

After a short conversation, he said, "Bunyard said they're leaving for the stockcar races, but he'll drop by for a look."

An old red pickup pulled up within minutes, and two men got out.

I introduced myself to James Bunyard and his son Al.

After Al inspected under the van, he said, "Daddy, we might have a drive shaft to fit back at the yard."

They soon returned with a drive shaft hanging out of the truck bed. Al connected the drive shaft as Mr. Bunyard stood stonily, sizing me up. He seemed to be a man of few words, so I didn't try to make small talk.

Al slid back out. "I believe you're ready to go."

Here was the moment of truth, "Mr. Bunyard, what do I owe you?"

"Well, the drive shaft is $100. You can pay whatever you want for our labor."

"Would you be happy with $150 total?"

He nodded.

"Mr. Bunyard, I don't have that much cash. Will you take a credit card?"

"We don't take cards."

"Will you take a check?"

He stiffened. "I don't like taking out-of-town checks. I've been burned too many times."

I stood taller. "Well, you don't know me, Sir, but I'm not going to write you a bad check with my son and nephew standing here as my witnesses."

He snorted as if he'd heard every sorry excuse ever made.

I handed him a copy of my first book, *Stories from the Creekbank*.

He turned it over in his hands. "You wrote that?"

"Yes, sir. That copy is for you."

Then I made my fatal mistake, handing him my business card:

Curt Iles

Manager

Dry Creek Baptist Camp

"Mr. Bunyard, I'm one of those good Baptists. You know I wouldn't cheat you."

I had just poured gasoline on the fire.

James Bunyard bolted right up, "Yep, I know all about you 'good Baptists.' Last year, a fellow broke down, and I got him going. He told me he was a *Baptist* preacher from Birmingham and would pay me on his next trip. As you can probably guess, I'm still waiting."

He scoffed, "Well, I guess I'll have to take your check."

My feathers were slightly ruffled. "Sir, somebody may have cheated you before, but it won't be this time."

He pointed a finger in my face. "Just remember that what goes around comes around."

I stiffened. "Mister Bunyard, I agree completely. This check will clear." I handed him the check. He looked at it like I'd given him a stack of Confederate dollars.

We shook hands, and they left in their truck for the stock car races. We resumed our westward trek on I-20.

As we drove away, Adam said, "Uncle Curt, he sure got worked up when you told him you were a good Baptist."

Clay pitched in, "Daddy, I don't believe your 'Baptist ID Card' was a good idea."

We laughed all the way to the Louisiana state line.

Later in the week, I called the bank to ensure the Bunyard check had cleared.

* * *

On a later I-20 trip, I visited the Bunyard's Transmission. Walking into the shop, I asked a worker, "I'm looking for James and Al."

He nodded toward a pair of feet sticking out from under a Chevrolet. "That's Al. Mr. James is gone today."

Al didn't recognize me as he stood up. I said, "I'm the Louisiana fellow you changed the drive shaft for last year."

A smile of recognition came over his face. "Yeah, you're the guy who wrote that book. Daddy's enjoyed your stories. I hate he's not here to see you."

I handed him several jars of homemade mayhaw jelly and two Dry Creek Camp caps, "I'll try to stop any time I'm in this neck of the woods." I hesitated at the door. "Al, one day, I'm going to put you and your Daddy in one of my books."

He grinned. "Oh, come on."

Reader, the book you're holding and the story you're reading is one more fulfilled promise to the Bunyards that I've kept.

A year later, I stopped in. You should have seen James Bunyard's face when I handed him a copy of *Wind in the Pines*. He thumbed through it, and I showed him "Watch Out for the Fish" and pointed out his name.

He was speechless, and I was happy. Once again, the ripple effect of my writing had traveled far from Dry Creek.

If you're traveling along the I-20 near the Alabama/Mississippi line, take Exit 165 for Toomsuba and drive south about one mile. You can't miss it on the right. Look for the sign that says, "No out-of-town checks accepted."

Tell them the Book-Man says, "Howdy, and thanks again."

I guarantee they'll help you in any way they can...

... but don't try to pass off an out-of-town check.

... Or tell them you're a Baptist.

Finally, if you've got a fish on the back of your car,

"D.L.J.W."

Drive like Jesus would.

Chapter 53

Glenda and Mr. Fox

I love April Fool's Day. I'm an unreformed prankster. I've pulled some fine pranks on April 1, and just as importantly, I've had a multitude of pranks on me. Don't dish it out if you can't take it.

The following is a fine April Fool's story:

Of all the teachers I worked with over the years, Glenda Hagan will always be one of my favorites.

She taught her entire career at East Beauregard, where she shaped two generations of English students and contributed greatly to our school's unique culture.

She loved pranking but was also one of the pretty gullible people, which made her so much fun to be around.

On this April Fool's Day, I was the assistant principal in our K-12 school.

I had my two unindicted co-conspirators, Carolyn and Bonnie, call her during her planning period.

"Mrs. Hagan, you have a call at the office."

I peeked from behind my office door when she came in.

Carolyn handed her the slip I'd carefully prepared:

Mr. Fox

Alexandria

(318) 441-6810.

Glenda took the note. "Who is Mr. Fox?"

Carolyn shrugged as Bonnie stuck her head around the door.

Glenda held the note to the light, "I don't know any Mr. Fox in Alexandria."

Finally, Glenda Hagan dutifully picked up the phone and dialed (318) 441-6810.

A cheerful voice answered, "Good morning, Alexandria Zoo."

Glenda Hagan paused. *"Uh, I have a note to call Mr. Fox."*

There was a long silence. "Ma'am, this is the Alexandria Zoo. It's April Fool's Day. I believe you've been pranked."

Glenda Hagan slammed down the phone, walked into the hallway, and yelled, "CURT ILES, I'M GOING TO KILL YOU!"

Evidently, she had a good idea who was behind the prank. She was a good sport about it but wagged a finger in my face. "Just remember: I will get you back."

And she was true to her word. Over the next year, I fell victim to many of her *revenge-pranks.* She's not the only one who's gullible.

When she'd stick the needle in, she'd remind me, "Remember Mr. Fox."

Happy April Fool's Day, Glenda. I cherish my years of working with you, but most of all, I'm privileged to call you my lifetime friend.

By the way, (318) 441-6810 is the actual Alexandria Zoo number. If you call today, ask for a list of the animal species prank calls they've received recently.

* * *

If you enjoyed "Mister Fox," you'll enjoy another pranking story in Chapter 56, "The Construction Worker."

Chapter 54

A Cup of Coffee with Mr. Bentley

"**J**onathan, did you have a cup of coffee this morning?"

My homeless friend grinned. "Yep. I got a hot cup from the Bentley."

"You got coffee from the *Hotel Bentley*?"

"Yeah, I slip in through a side door each morning, and the workers serve me a cup."

I smile. "So you really had coffee at the Bentley?"

"Yes, it was Folger's, and it was good and hot."

I shake my head. *I wonder what Joseph Bentley would have thought.*

* * *

Joseph Bentley, a timber baron from Pennsylvania, arrived in Alexandria in 1908 during the heyday of the vast cutover of Louisana's longleaf forest. After a hard day tromping through the woods, Joseph Bentley was denied dinner service at an Alexandria hotel due to his "dress and lack of proper attire."

Joseph Bentley didn't take this slight lying down. He supposedly vowed, "I will build a hotel that will put yours to shame and hopefully also put you out of business."

That's how the majestic Hotel Bentley along the Red River came to be. It is considered the finest hotel between Memphis and New Orleans—a classic Renaissance-style five-story hotel built primarily of marble.

Every visitor to Alexandria should visit its lobby. It is breathtaking, with chandeliers, mural frescoes on the ceiling, and a grand ballroom—it reminds me of photos of the Palace of Versailles.□

Walking in, I'm transported back to the Red River cotton boom or antebellum New Orleans during the height of the steamboat era. I can nearly smell the cigar smoke and echoes from the once-crowded lobby.

Over the last fifty years, the Bentley has gone through tough times of closure and new ownership, but you'd never know it as you stand in the lobby.

Behind the lobby, there's a legendary room where Generals Eisenhower, Patton, Bradley, and Krueger purportedly dissected the 1941 Louisiana Maneuvers and began laying the groundwork for the coming war in Europe.

Joseph Bentley lived in his hotel until he died in 1913. There's a portrait of him in the lobby. I always tip my cap in passing. I'd like to ask him what he thought about a homeless man slipping in the side door each morning for a steaming cup of java.

It's just my imagination, but I'd swear I detected a slight smile as I passed his portrait.

Joseph Bentley.

He built a historic hotel that oversees downtown Alexandria, where I work.

The Hotel Bentley.

You've got to see it to believe it.

While you're there, ask for a steaming cup of coffee and tell them it's on the house.

The house Joseph Bentley built.

Chapter 55

The Outsider

S he's now known as Queen Mary, the ultimate Dry Creek insider.

I call her Momma. She's Mary Iles, my 89-year-old mother.

Everybody in Dry Creek knows her, and everyone in Dry Creek loves her. She's the ultimate insider.

But it wasn't always so.

When my parents moved to the country in 1960, the Dry Creek community was still a closed society.

My mother, who'd always lived in small towns, was now in the midst of this close-cropped culture, an area still suspicious of outsiders.

Dry Creek was made up of pine plantations owned by big timber companies. Amid the miles of pines were small landowners or clans that had settled years earlier. At that time, most people in Dry Creek were kin or longtime residents.

My mom had married into a Dry Creek family, but she wasn't from here.

Some folks moved in and never fit in or were accepted.

Momma started out that way. It'd be easy to crawl into a hole.

But that wasn't Mary Iles's way.

Here are some of the many hats she's worn in a lifetime in Dry Creek.

The Travel Agent

She loaded my sisters and me up in our old truck and, if it cranked, hit the road, making a conscious decision to get out and meet people.

Mom came from a great family, but they were always on the move with the railroad. She attended multiple schools throughout her childhood. I think that one of the reasons why, when we got to Dry Creek, she wanted us rooted. We weren't going to move around like her childhood.

We were going to grow up in Dry Creek, and there couldn't have been a better place or time.

Recently, I asked her, "Mom, why in the world did you move out here in the middle of nowhere to live at the dead end of a dirt road in a log house with no indoor plumbing?"

"Well, it took your Daddy six years to talk me into moving out here to the *sticks*. It was never my idea, but when we got here, I decided to make the most of it."

She still refers to where we live as the sticks. It was her definition of the vast pine plantations and hardwood swamp that surrounded us.

It's what I call the woods.

The Germans called it the hinterlands: "Beyond the land."

The middle of nowhere.

It's where I come from.

All I know is that it was a great place to grow up.

All of us, especially Mom, began to find her place.

I've heard people say, "Well, I moved into a place, and no one was friendly."

Find you a church.

"But none of the churches are friendly."

Then, find one that is or join some local group or club.

Mom's attitude was to carry her own sunshine with her. It's hard to be shunned or ignored if you're friendly.

In other words, "If you like people, people will like you."

She threw herself into various church activities, including Vacation Bible School and the W.M.U. (Women's Missionary Union) and she always taught one of the children's Sunday School classes.

Even at a young age, I began to realize she was irresistible. You couldn't help but like her.

It didn't hurt that she was beautiful. She'd been Most Beautiful at DeRidder High School, and she was one good-looking woman. Even as a youngster, I realized I had a good-looking mother. I'll get in hot water for saying it, but she was, in today's parlance, "My Momma was *hot.*"

She may no longer be "hot," but she's still beautiful at 89.

Mom's beauty was never about outward appearances. She has an inner beauty that mirrors her personal relationship with God.

* * *

Mom wasn't content to sit at the dead end of a one-mile dirt road. If it were a day she had the truck and could crank it, she'd load us up in the truck bed and haul us to civilization.

I'll let her tell one of her best stories:

"One day, I pulled up to Ryan Harper's Grocery in the back of our backfiring truck with about a half-dozen neighbor kids and at least four yapping dogs.

Mr. Ryan walked to the truck bed, which was alive with tangled kids and dogs, and nodded, 'Now, Mary, I want to warn you: If you keep hauling those dogs in the back of your truck, they'll follow you off and get run over.'

This was years before seat belts and car seats.

Curt, I still laugh at Ryan Harper's concerns about the dogs, but paying no attention to the gaggle of kids hanging off the truck bed.

It was a different time.

I can't believe I let you and the girls ride in the bed of the truck."

Walt Disney Meets the Bookmobile

Two stories stand out about my mom's commitment to my sisters and me.

I call one "Walt Disney" and the other "The Bookmobile."

We were the proverbial family that if the church doors were open, we were there.

That meant twice on Sunday and Wednesday night prayer meetings. I always wondered why we had to go to church twice on the Sabbath, the supposed day of rest.

Sunday night meant Training Union followed by another full service.

I recall the adage, "I'd be a Baptist, too, if I could hold up to it."

The biggest problem was Sunday night. Training Union meant we missed Walt Disney, which was a great source of pain for Colleen and me.

That week, Momma wrote Walt Disney. She explained to him the problem with her children and Training Union, asking if the time of the show could be moved to a different time slot for church kids.

A month later, she received *a personal note* from Walt Disney.

I was learning to read, so Mom showed it to me.

She read it aloud.

Dear Mrs. Iles,

Thank you for your letter.

I understand your concern about the time slot for Walt Disney World.

This decision is made by the network and sponsors, not our company.

Thank you again for your letter.

It was hand-signed by Walt Disney.

I rubbed my hand over the great man's signature. Even as a youngster, I understood that Walt Disney probably didn't personally sign it. Still, the realization that someone had taken the time to reply to P.O. Box 322 Dry Creek, Louisiana, made a lasting impression on me.

I also knew that my sweet mom would move Heaven and Earth and the World of Walt Disney for my sisters and me.

I still believe she still would.

The Bookmobile

A memorable story of her commitment to our education was her crusade to bring the Bookmobile to Dry Creek.

Our rural location at the dead end of a dirt road is the reason I still smile about the day the Bookmobile came to our house.

We moved to Dry Creek (from DeRidder) when I was four. We lived in the Old House for a year while my parents built a house nearby. When we moved into our new house, Daddy named it "Poverty Knob," much to Momma's displeasure.

Not long after that, the Beauregard Parish Library Bookmobile made its first trip to our home.

I've always wondered what strings Momma had to pull to get the library van to come to our house each summer. We were far off the beaten path, with just my sister Colleen and me as patrons (my sister Claudia was a baby).

Our road could become nearly impassable during muddy weather. More than once, we got stuck. To call it a gravel road was a gross exaggeration; it was a dirt road... which "rutted up" after a rain.

I'll never forget these trips to the Bookmobile. I'd sit on the front steps, awaiting its arrival. Hearing it coming up the last hill before our house, I knew it was it. No one ever came down our road unless they were coming to see us or were lost.

The Bookmobile was coming to see us.

I recall the feel of the hot sand as I ran barefoot to the Bookmobile's steps. The cool interior of the air-conditioned Bookmobile quickly offset the hot Louisiana humidity.

I was determined to take advantage of every bit of the cold air. With Momma's help, we went through the shelves, selecting books. It was such a happy time in my childhood.

The library lady would kindly remind us that she had to leave in "a few minutes." We'd wait as long as possible to leave the cool confines of the Bookmobile.

Carrying an armload of books, we stepped back out into the June heat and waved as the Bookmobile disappeared around the curve, leaving a cloud of dust.

I knew it would be back in two weeks, and then I would trade my stack of books for another one.

It has a definite connection in my heart. My mom made sure we had every opportunity to learn, grow, and read.

It was a gift she gave to us.

To me, arranging for the Bookmobile to come to Poverty Knob was a strong sign of how strong that love was.

This opportunity to get free books for reading left an impression on me. I believe it was the beginning of my passionate love of reading and later writing career.

Branson or Bust

Recently, Momma pulled a fast one on me.

"Curt, you promised to take me to Branson for my 90th birthday."

"Momma, *I did no such thing*. I told you last time we went that *I wouldn't be going back*."

"But you promised . . . "

"Momma, there's no way I promised to take you to Branson. You're past going, and I have no business taking you."

"But you promised me . . ."

It's hard to win an argument with an eighty-nine-year-old, especially if she's your mother,

Resistance is futile. She wore me down, mentioning Branson on every visit.☐
   You guessed it. In March, we're going to Branson, Missouri, and I'm reconciled to taking her. In fact, I'm excited about the trip. If I have to haul her in a wheelbarrow to see the Baldknobbers, Lord willing, we're going.

If she drops dead during the March Branson trip, she will die happy.

And I've always wanted her to be happy.

* * *

Branson has always been Mom's holy Mecca. She and Daddy went dozens of times, often seeing three shows in one day. I've told her that when she dies, St. Peter will give her a day pass to Branson before she reaches the Pearly Gates.

I just hope it's not in March 2025.

The Cruise Director

"Curt, you can't have too many friends."

—Momma's sage advice over the years

Momma has always been able to work a crowd as smoothly as Bill Clinton. There's nothing shallow about it; she really enjoys meeting people.

It's Mom's 89th birthday, and thirty of her family are celebrating it at Roy's Catfish in Kinder.

I guide her on a walker to her seat of honor at the end of one of two long tables. She is surrounded by her children, grandchildren, great-grandchildren, and special friends.

I take my seat at the other end and begin scanning the menu. I look up.

Mom has left her chair walker-less and is making her way around the tables, speaking to each person, patting their shoulder, and smiling.

She grips the chairs for stability as she smiles and greets each guest, regardless of age.

I nudge my son Clint. "There she is, still being the cruise director at 89."

We laugh. That's who she is.

She wants to invite everyone into the warm circle of her friendship.

I've watched her do it, with all sincerity, since we moved to Dry Creek in 1960.

That's how you go from being The Outsider to the Queen Mother of Dry Creek.

At some point in her early decades of country living, she began introducing herself as "I'm Mary Iles from Dry Creek."

My mother, Queen Mary, who lives in the brown wood frame house at the end of Clayton Iles Road.

"Hello, I'm Mary Iles from Dry Creek."

I figured if she could be proud of being from Dry Creek, so could I.

.

Chapter 56

The Construction Worker

A s you learned earlier in "Mister Fox," I love a good prank.

Before I share my all-time favorite prank, I want to add a disclaimer:

A prank should never harm a person, physically or emotionally. Example: no snakes! A prank should be *laughable* on both ends and is never meant to embarrass someone.

. . . and the prankster must be ready to be pranked three-fold in return. In other words, don't dish it out if you can't take it. Be prepared to be a good sport when it circles back to you.

* * *

The following story will always be my best prank.

A school's morale needs to have some fun along with solid instruction. One morning, when I was principal at EBHS, I arrived at school early before the custodians or lunchroom workers arrived.

I carried a pair of my mud-caked rubber boots in the *faculty* women's bathroom and locked myself in the single stall.

You need some background before I continue.

Construction was going on a building extension for the high school. In their comings and goings, the workers tracked in mud. The custodians constantly complained about the workers making a mess in the hallways and bathrooms.

That's why I stood locked inside the women's faculty bathroom, holding a pair of muddy rubber boots.

I placed the boots in front of the commode. I brought two short sticks and a pair of ratty jeans.

I inserted the sticks in the boots and arranged/draped the blue jeans over the sticks.

I carefully arranged the jeans in the posture of someone sitting on the throne. For added realism, I set a roll of toilet paper between the boots and shook a little caked mud.

I couldn't stop laughing as I made a final inspection of my handiwork.

Then, I did the most challenging part of my project. Holding my necktie, I crawled out from under the stall door. It was a tight fit. I sure couldn't do it now.

I leaned against the sink, admiring my artwork. From the outside, it looked just like one of the construction workers on the commode.

Don't forget this was the one-stall ladies' bathroom.

I hurried to my office. No one else knew my secret.

As school started, I was busy with the chores of a K-12 principal: a bus driver bringing in a rowdy fourth-grader or a red-faced parent while signing a stack of excused absences.

I signed tardy slips as the morning announcements were broadcast. I kept my eyes on the hallway, waiting to see who'd report the construction worker stuck in the women's restroom.

Nearly an hour passed before the four custodians met me at my office door.

Thelma Bushnell was naturally the spokesperson. I loved Mrs. Thelma dearly, but she could be a bit bossy and a tad nosey. Sometimes, I wondered if she was working for me or if I was working for her.

She said, "Mr. Iles, one of those construction workers, has been in the women's restroom for nearly an hour."

"What?"

"Yes, he's been in there. We keep checking on him, but he's still there."

"Did y'all speak to him?"

"No, but Sugar heard him grunt."

I nearly lost it.

"Mr. Iles, you need to come see for yourself."

The committee led me to the bathroom. "See there."

I shook my head. "Do you think he's all right?"

"As quiet as he is, he might have passed out or might be dead."

"Or he's got a major-league case of constipation."

Once again, I nearly lost it.

I bent over. "Sir, are you all right?"

Crickets.

I shook the door. It's locked.

"Fellow, just let me know you're in there."

I turned to Kelly. "Go get a chair, and we'll look over the door to check on him."

He returned and stood on the chair for a bird's eye view. I'm not positive, but I believe he cursed under his breath.

The next custodian took her turn on the chair.

"Mr. Iles, I cannot believe you did that! You ought to have more to do than playing pranks."

"How do you know I did it?"

"Because I know you, and this was right up your alley. We will get you back. Just watch and see."

I now had the thankless job of crawling back under the stall and unlocking the door.

They gathered in admiration of my setup.

Thelma Bushnell said, "Mr. Iles, you really don't have enough to do, do you?"

Sugar said, "Where in the world did you get this crazy idea?"

"From my Uncle Bill, the world's finest prankster."

It still is my all-time favorite prank.

Those four custodians repeatedly pranked me over the remaining school year, and we laughed together each time.

Chapter 57

Shake Like a Man

I 'm writing a book entitled *The Pineywoods Manifesto: Field Notes to Life*. You can help shape this future book. We'd love your input (yes, you're part of the project) in writing this important book.

It's written for my four grandsons and contains stories, wisdom, and timeless values from the culture I grew up in. Although I'm writing it for Noah, Jack, Jude, and Luke, I believe *A Pineywoods Manifesto* will be applicable to every person, male or female.

I'd be so honored if you shared the bedrock lessons that have shaped your life. We'd love to hear from you at creekbank.stories@gmail.com.

I encourage you to model these core qualities with all of the young people in your circle of influence.

In fact, it'd be good for us adults to brush up on the common courtesies of life that seem to be becoming less common. Because it's never out of style to be a gentleman.

Here's my favorite chapter so far.

Shake like a Man

Every rural community has at least one of them—the man who has the nutcracker handshake.

Tubby King filled that role in Dry Creek. He was a human vise grip.

When I was a young teenager, Tubby and Agnes King joined our church. I soon learned a valuable lesson about Tubby. He had a vise-grip handshake and would hurt your hand if you didn't get a good grip.

I'd been taught how to shake hands like a man earlier in life.

It's a proactive, slightly aggressive move where you ensure you get the webbed area between your thumb and forefinger right against the same part of the *shakee,* or fellow shaker's. If you do this, you'll get a firm grip, and guys like Tubby can't squeeze your fingers like wringing out a wet dishrag.

I don't think Tubby King meant to hurt other men with his handshake. He was a fine man who would always give a tearful testimony of how good God had been to him, but his handshake brought tears to a generation of Dry Creek men and boys.

His handshake was hurtful *only* if you didn't know how to shake like a man.

It's a learned habit.

Extend your right hand in a friendly, forceful manner and give a firm handshake. It's not a contest of the tightest grip, but men in the Louisiana Pineywoods (and much of the world) are judged by their handshake.

You don't have to go to CrossFit to have a firm handshake. It's available to every man and boy,

There's no place for a dead fish handshake in our culture.

No wet dishrags.

No limp or wimpy ones.

Just as a firm shake gives an impressive impression, a limp handshake gives the opposite impression. There's no room in the Christian Kingdom of Men for wimpy handshakes.

In our world travels on missions, I was introduced to several variations. On the African Continent, it's common to place your left hand on your right forearm during the handshake. It shows that the shaker isn't holding a weapon behind his back with the free hand. As we'd say, "Etu, Brute."

I learned another handshake variation in Indonesia in the aftermath of the terrible 2004 Tsunami. I led a Louisiana medical team that ministered to the refugees from this century's worst natural disaster. The Indonesian Sumatrans would shake my hand while patting their heart with their left hand, saying, "Thank you for coming in our time of need."

The hand to the chest was explained as their way of adding, "I am connected to your heart." Coming from the deeply Muslim people of Aceh, I always took this symbolic gesture literally to heart.

Worldwide, the handshake is a symbolic feature of introduction and connection.

So, shake like a man. You don't have to be a bodybuilder to have a firm handshake. It's just a matter of practice and technique.

It's part of a good first impression. It can also open doors to strong friendships, jobs, and lifetime opportunities.

So, shake like a man.

Tubby's real name was Lester King, and he had a twin brother named Chester. I've always wondered if his brother Chester had a handshake to match Tubby.

I've always been too afraid to find out.

* * *

There's another type of manly handshake that is reserved for special people and times. There's a higher level of handshaking that isn't taught but is always genuine. I call it "The Clasp."

"Coach." That's what Duane Watson always calls me, and it's a name I proudly answer to. It's a strong word reserved for special relationships.

I'm visiting my home church, Dry Creek Baptist Church, and we're having communion.

Duane is one of the deacons passing the communion plate. When he reaches my row, I take my wafer and pass the plate down the row.

He extends his hand and grasps mine in the firm handshake that I'm sure his father, Uncle Joe Watson, taught him. Then Duane does something else. He clasps his left hand over mine.

I return the favor and place my left hand over his. It's called the clasp.

Our clasp says more than a thousand words could say about how we feel about each other.

That clasp is firm and doesn't need words. Duane and I lock eyes in a wordless dialogue.

It's literally heart-warming, and there's nothing squirrely about it.

No man who has ever been in a clasp like this would call it that.

It's the respectful hand clasp of two men who don't mind openly sharing their mutual love and respect.

It's a *four-handed-man's-handshake.*

A clasp of the hands and heart.

Duane loosens his grip and continues down the aisle. Hot tears sting my eyes, but I'm not embarrassed. A handshake like that ought to touch a man deeply.

I can still feel it—wordless but powerful beyond words.

In fact, a week later, I still felt it.

I don't believe the clasp can be scripted or even planned. It just happens. That's what a real man's handshake does. That's what's exchanged when you shake like a man and look him in the eyes.

Chapter 58

The Quiet Sheriff

*F*riday, *September 23, 2005*

DeRidder, Louisiana

10:00 AM Central Daylight time

Day 0 for the arrival of Hurricane Rita

It was ten hours before Hurricane Rita would slam into Southwest Louisiana. A crowded room of Beauregard Parish officials and citizens listened intently as emergency preparedness leaders reviewed last-minute plans for the upcoming storm.

As the meeting wound down, the leader said, "Sheriff, would you like to say a word?"

Bolivar Bishop had been Beauregard Parish sheriff for thirty-four years. He'd long ago won the respect and confidence of every man and woman in the room.

From his spot against the back wall, Sheriff Bishop calmly said, "I appreciate how everyone has worked together to get ready.

"Don't worry; there won't be any Katrina-type looting here. Our people will help take care of your roads and homes."

There wasn't even a chair squeaking in the room as Sheriff Bishop finished, "We'll get through this together. We'll come out of this all right,"

No one said a word.

No one moved.

The sheriff had spoken.

I believed him. We would come out of this all right and work together in the days and months ahead.

Yes. Bolivar Bishop was my sheriff—the epitome of quiet leadership.

I've studied leaders and leadership for my entire life, and Bolivar Bishop is still one of the best examples of a "Quiet Leader" I've known.

He was soft-spoken, but when he spoke, people listened.

That's the mark of a leader. A real leader has earned the respect of those around him, especially those who work with him.

Sheriff Bishop was a man of stability and calm. It would be a mistake to view this quietness as a weakness. He understood his position.

To me, he always seemed comfortable in his own skin.

In Louisiana, the Parish Sheriff has always been one of the most powerful officials in the parish and the state. A local sheriff has outsized authority.

Sheriff Bishop exercised that authority in a positive way.

I was always intrigued by Sheriff Bishop's leadership style. When he was first elected in 1971, he was a banker with no law enforcement background. He served nine terms, usually with no opposition.

He preferred to be in the background. He surrounded himself with able deputies and administrators, got out of their way, and allowed them to do their jobs.

That's another trait of an effective leader—they are not afraid to delegate authority.

They have the self-confidence to realize the entire world doesn't have to revolve around them.

They're in charge but have no reason to flaunt their authority.

Bolivar Bishop didn't have to flaunt his power. He was comfortable with it and used his position to improve our parish.

He was the epitome of the Quiet Leader.

And he was my sheriff.

And you know what?

I guess he always will be.

Chapter 59

The Lost Boy

"Grief. I don't think you ever work through it. Grief and loss are things that
never go away. They stay with you."

-Keanu Reeves

I'm not sure there is a more profound sadness than the tragic death of a child.

It often leads to a lifetime of what-ifs, "If only . . . "

My Uncle Clint: I often wonder what he would've been like now. I know we
would've been close friends.

I often think about his short life because I've observed for a lifetime how his life
and death affected everything about my generations of the Iles clan.

The following is an excerpt from Harold Kushner's *How Good Do We Have to
Be?*

Kushner writes, *"The Missing Piece,* a children's book by Shel Silverstein, is the
story of a circle from which a large rectangular wedge has been cut.

"The circle wants to be whole, so it goes looking for the missing piece. But
because it is incomplete, it can only roll slowly. Along the way, it admires the
flowers, chats with butterflies, and enjoys the sunshine.,

"It found lots of pieces, but none fit. So, it left them on the side of the road and
kept on searching.

"Then, one day, it found a piece that fit exactly. It was so happy. Now, it could be whole, with nothing missing. But as a perfect circle, it rolled too fast to notice the flowers or talk to the butterflies."

Rabbi Kushner, who had lost his son to cancer, commented, "We are more whole when we are incomplete. The tragedies and trials of life cause us to slow down and love and appreciate what is around us."

In our family, the missing piece occurred on December 3, 1958, with the tragic death of my Uncle Clint. As I write this, it has been over sixty-five years since his loss.

As I write this, I feel very inadequate and unworthy to be the one to put into words my feelings for my uncles, aunts, and parents.

However, it is essential to remember and express our feelings. And I do feel that I am the one to write this. Even though I only vaguely remember Clint, I think about him often. He was six, and I was two. Because of my age as the oldest member of my generation, I understand a little of the deep feelings held by those older than me.

Here's why I'm writing "The Lost Boy," I want my Uncle Clint Iles's life to be remembered. If I don't tell his story, he will be lost to memory, history, and a small headstone in Beauregard Cemetery.

As dates pass and events occur in my family, I wonder what Clint would be like today. Because of our close ages, I often wonder what we would have enjoyed doing together. He was in a family of creative eccentrics. I wonder if he'd been one or both. I wonder.

How he would have left his mark on this world.

And then I am reminded of how he left his mark in six short years. Reading the story of the missing piece, I realize how Clint's life and untimely death changed my family. Although these changes were deeply sad, beyond words, and deeply personal, I want to dwell on a positive thing that came out of this.

I speak for myself, my sisters, and my cousins when I describe how our uncles and aunts treated us. No one ever received more encouragement, attention, and love from their relatives than the seven of us did. I grew up in a loving family environment. Everywhere I looked, I was surrounded by loving family.

Back then, I didn't understand the word clan. That's how I would describe us: the Iles clan, and like clans do, we stuck together.

I believe the loss of our Uncle Clint enhanced this love. The loss of this precious missing piece in our family only made everyone love each other.

Let me be clear: It wasn't easy, and at times, it was a sad love. I would sometimes sense that sadness in the eyes of my family members. Those same uncles and aunts, along with their spouses, invested in my life.

When I think about Clint, I most often think of his mother, my precious MaMa. I doubt if there is any pain worse than a mother tragically losing a child. As the years passed, MaMa turned her grief into a deep spiritual walk with Jesus and a lifetime of unselfishly taking care of everyone but herself.

I was nervous when, in 1984, I suggested to MaMa that we name our second son, Clint. Her beautiful blue eyes lit up, and tears rolled down her cheeks. "I'd like that."

In the final season of her life, she had a stroke that left her mute, but those bright blue eyes and her smile spoke volumes.

I sat beside her a few weeks before she died. I pointed at a photo of Uncle Clint above her bed. "MaMa, do you think about how you'll see Clint soon?"

She gripped my hand, and her eyes seemed a million miles away. She smiled and nodded. No words were said, and none were needed.

It's the last time I saw those beautiful blue eyes.

In his memoir *Journeyman*, my Uncle Bill Iles shares about the death of his younger brother:

The Lost Boy:

"On December 3, 1958, my six-year-old brother Clint was struck by a car and killed crossing Bon Ami Street, which separated our house from the DeRidder Elementary School, which had let out for the day. I arrived home and passed Clint, who was already home from school, safe and sound, playing on the front lawn on my way inside the house. Between that perfect moment and my baby brother's death, Clint remembered the book satchel he left at school. Clint, a child lost in thought and sure in familiar territory so near the safety of home and school, didn't see the oncoming car as he was crossing the street.

In an instant, Clint's head hit the curb hard. My mother, alerted to the crisis by my grandmother's piercing scream, rushed to Clint's lifeless body, picked him up, and held him in her arms; he sighed once and died.

Clint was taken to the emergency room but never regained consciousness; He died on Bon Ami in our mother's arms. No heartfelt prayers could save him.

The tragedy of Clint's death had a profound effect on each member of our family. It brought us closer together, united as we were in our sense of grief and loss.

* * *

A moment from my own father's funeral is seared into my memory.

In the rural South, the friends pass by the casket to pay their final respects. Usually, the casket is opened for what is called the final viewing.

As a younger man, I viewed this part of the service as ghoulish and time-consuming, but as I conducted dozens of funerals and stood at the head of the casket, I began to see it in a new light.

As I watched the compassionate interaction of cherished friends with the family members, I realized this was a necessary and healthy part of the grieving process. Folks were able to say goodbye in their own personal way.

Invariably, as the line snaked between the casket and seated family, someone would stop and go to the bereaved, and the entire line would slow to a crawl as nearly every following friend gave a hug or a word.

But that was important, too. You never forget who attended the funeral of a loved one, and the long line of mourners was part of that.

Daddy had a fine funeral, just as he deserved. There was an extremely long line filing by his casket. I noticed movement behind me and turned to see my uncle and aunts approach an older woman at the casket.

It was Mrs. Heard.

Mrs. Heard was driving the car that hit Uncle Clint. The accident wasn't her fault, and none of our family ever blamed her. In fact, it formed an unspoken unbreakable bond between our two families.

I watched my elders, standing in front of their eldest brother's casket, hugging Mrs. Heard. She had grieved all these years like the rest of us. She was a part of our family, united by sorrow and trial but firmly knotted.

I was never prouder of the kind of people I come from.

* * *

My Uncle Bill is now eighty and still producing the best paintings of his long career. Outwardly, he was most affected by the death of his younger brother.

Uncle Bill is a renowned artist and my favorite uncle. He recently had a large art show at a Lake Charles gallery, where over sixty of his paintings, journals, and artifacts were tastefully displayed.

Many of his large landscape murals are hung. This is my favorite period of his work: dark, brooding bayous and sunlight on Pineywoods roads.

A large crowd attended the opening of his last show. As they snaked around the exhibits, one painting held the most attention.

It was Uncle Bill's large collage painting of Uncle Clint's death. It is centered on my grandmother holding Clint's lifeless body. It depicts the anguish and sadness of the family: Clint's grandparents, his dad, and his siblings are forever etched around MaMa and Uncle Clint.

Each plays a part in the grim story.

The art show crowd, reading the placeholder with Uncle Bill's description of the painting, was mesmerized. They couldn't leave it. It was as if that painting was reaching out and grabbing them by the heart, making them part of our family's long-held grief.

Occasionally, someone would ask Uncle Bill to come and explain the story and scenes. It moved me to watch him. He'd poured out his grief on his canvas.

And I prayed that as he shared, that hole in his heart from December 1958 would be filled.

The following week, I took my granddaughter to the exhibit. Uncle Bill took time to explain and set the scene for all of his works. It was one of the best days of my life.

We walked to Uncle Clint's painting. "Uncle Bill, tell me what each part represents."

He had glued in school papers from his brother's first-grade notebook.

I was deeply moved.

I'm moved even now.

I thought of my relationship with my uncle. He is a big brother, elder uncle, and father figure in my life.

None of my family ever said it, but I believe that as the oldest child of the next generation, I took Uncle Clint's place in their hearts. No one could take his place, but I believe my age and resemblance filled a little corner of that dark void. My great-grandfather always called me "Clint" before correcting it to Curt. He called me that until the day he died.

No one else could replace him, and I didn't try to. Maybe, in a way, I was that piece of the wheel and partially fit the hole and allowed it to move forward.

I'm nearly sixty-eight now. Uncle Clint would be seventy-two. The Lost Boy's been gone for over sixty years.

Many have forgotten he lived.

I never will.

I guess that's the real reason I wrote this.

His name was David Clinton Iles. Clinton David Iles.

And he was my uncle.

My Uncle Clint.

David Clinton Iles

1952-1958

Chapter 60

Friend-Collecting

There was a fine crowd at Joe Chaney's funeral and just as many at his wake the night the night before.

Both crowds in the Camp Tabernacle consisted of country people. That's because Joe Chaney was a country man, and these were *his* people.

And that's no sin. Being country.

Leaving the wake, I took notice there were many more trucks than cars.

I was among *my* people.

I had the privilege of giving the eulogy at Joe's service. It was a fine funeral replete with many fine stories and plenty of laughter through the tears.

It's the only funeral I've been to where rooster fighting was mentioned.

Only in Dry Creek.

Joe's stepson Trey shared how Joe had assured him that Jesus was his Savior. Trey's description of his stepdad deeply moved me. Let me correct that: Trey didn't speak of Joe Chaney as a stepfather. It was the warm embrace of family that cannot be broken.

When it was my time, I scanned the large crowd from the stage. "If I'm correct, there's not one man here today with a necktie."

A whisper of laughter.

"Except Joe."

More laughter.

"Now, let me make it clear. Joe's not wearing a tie in the casket. He's got his work shirt on."

I nodded at the large portrait of Joe beside his casket. "Joe Chaney's got a necktie on. He's the only one here with one on.

"Linda said the portrait came from a photo taken of Joe on a cruise. You had to wear a tie to get to the buffet. That's probably about the only thing that could get a tie on Joe. A long line of king crab legs, shrimp, and steak will do it to any man."

I closed my remarks. Looking at the crowd of men and women, I said, "Joe Chaney had lots of jobs in his life, but his real job was collecting: he was a friend-collector."

There was a murmur of agreement from the crowd.

I'm going to miss Joe Chaney when the first copies of *Where I Come From* arrive. He was an avid reader of anything I wrote, and I always ensured he got one of the first copies.

Joe and Linda ran Foreman's Grocery, so I saw Joe several times weekly. He'd be waiting for me, ready to discuss his current favorite stories. I took his reviews very seriously. Joe came from two legendary branches of the finest Louisiana country storytellers I've known: the Chaney and Cady families.

Yes, he was my friend.

A real friend-collector.

* * *

Before leaving, I'd like to get in a word edgewise:

A true friend-collector doesn't just make friends; he keeps them.

And there is a difference.

I want to do that in my life. I want to be a friend-collector and a friend-keeper.

I've been blessed. Many of my closest friends are still men I grew up with in Dry Creek. I've tried to be a friend-keeper, putting them in the pocket of my shirt close to my heart.

Being a friend-collector and friend-keeper. It sounds like a fine job description. I think I'll apply for an official position.

Chapter 61

A Mentor Named Fox Conner

H e wasn't from Louisiana, but Fox Conner was a true Southern man.

Although he is largely forgotten, he played a vital role in the lives of some of our most famous military leaders in World War II.

I've always been fascinated with leadership.

I'm drawn to military leaders, and Fox Conner is one of those names.

What a fine first name.

It wasn't a nickname.

Fox Conner.

His father, Robert Conner, fought in the Civil War and was blinded at the Battle of Atlanta. The Conner family had deep roots in Mississippi, where Fox Conner spent his boyhood.

You've probably never heard of Major General Fox Conner. He had an outstanding career spanning the Spanish-American War through the post-World War I years.

Three names mark him as a *remarkable mentor:* George C. Patton, George C. Marshall, and Dwight Eisenhower.

Fox Conner had the skill of bonding with young officers as a mentor and friend.

It started with an officer named George S. Patton. They met on a train before the First World War. General Conner became a lifetime mentor and friend to Patton, guiding him in what true leadership is.

***

During the First World War, George C. Marshall served under Fox Conner's command. Once again, General Conner taught and modeled what it meant to be an American military leader. General Marshall later led America's two-front war effort to defeat Nazi Germany and Imperial Japan. Marshall also served as Secretary of State and authored the post-war "Marshall Plan" that saved Western Europe from starvation and communism.

George Marshall referred to his time with Fox Conner as "life-shaping."

***

But Fox Conner's most memorable mentorship took place in Panama with a young, charismatic colonel named Dwight D. Eisenhower.

Eisenhower was at a low point in his life and career when he met Fox Conner. He and his wife Mamie had recently lost a son. Careerwise, the years between the Wars were a desert for career officers like him.

General Conner, who was leading American forces in the Canal Zone, took Eisenhower and his family under his wing during their three years together in Panama.

He put "Ike" on a strict regimen of reading and studying military and world history, as well as military doctrine and planning.

Fox Conner modeled for Dwight Eisenhower how to lead, delegate, and work closely with Allies.

I don't need to expand on the pivotal place General Eisenhower played in leading the Allies to victory over Nazi Germany.

After the War, an interviewer asked Eisenhower, "You've served with the top generals and world leaders. Who would you name as the greatest one you worked with?

Dwight Eisenhower replied without hesitation. "Fox Conner."

Eisenhower later commented on Conner's abilities: "Outside of my parents, he had more influence on me and my outlook than any other individual, especially in regard to the military profession."

Fox Conner mentored three of the towering figures of the 20th Century. His name is worth remembering.

* * *

Conner had three principles or rules of War for a Democracy that he imparted to Eisenhower, Marshall, and Patton.

- Never fight unless you have to;

- Never fight alone;

- And never fight for long.

* * *

Fox Conner approached life as a mentor.

Mentor. Now, there's a fine word. It's defined as "a trusted counselor or guide."

Mentorship involves taking a younger person under your arm and walking beside them on this part of their journey. Age has nothing to do with it, nor does gender or level of education. Mentorship goes well beyond race and status.

Mentorship doesn't have to be formal. Often, it's a bond that occurs naturally. It takes time, presence, and an understanding that leadership is *caught, not taught*.

Anyone reading this can become a mentor. I encourage you to look around for younger men or women who have potential and promise. You might make *a world of difference.*

If you asked me at this season what has been the most fulfilling part of my life, I'd reply, "Mentoring and leading young men."

I've been privileged as a father to three boys, a teacher, coach, principal, camp manager, and an African missionary. In each of my diverse careers, one thing has been consistent: the opportunity to rub elbows with young men and pour into their lives.

Many have become lifetime friends. I've rejoiced at their successes and wept with them in their setbacks. They have mentored me as much, maybe more, as my mentorship to them.

I am a man most blessed.

* * *

Much of the information on Fox Conner comes from the excellent book *Grey Eminence: Fox Conner and the Art of Mentorship* by Edward L. Cox.

Chapter 62

A Broken Cup

Your deepest pain can give you the highest platform.

When my favorite coffee cup fell onto the patio floor, it shattered, and shards scattered about. The handle broke off, and a sizeable crescent-shaped piece of the rim was gone. Sadly, it would now only hold three sips of coffee.

I really liked its rough ceramic finish and how it kept my coffee hot, but now it was useless. I walked to the trash can . . . and then stopped.

Instead of tossing the cup, I retrieved a Sharpie and wrote across the bottom: *I've been broken, but I'm still useful.*

I can understand that because I've been broken, too.

My brokenness comes from periodic bouts of deep depression.

Many times during those dark times, I felt as if I was broken beyond repair. My depression was so deep, dark, and long that I doubted that I'd survive or ever be of use again.

However, I was wrong; In God's economy, nothing is wasted. He takes everything in our lives and shapes us to be more useful for the Kingdom. So, in spite of my dark valleys, I'm still useful. The fact that you're reading this book means God can still use broken people.

My depression has made me a better and more empathic man, and it's given me a platform and voice to encourage others suffering from this illness.

Those of you who've been with me through my previous books will notice a difference in my writing.

I've been broken and put back together again.

That changes everything about a man, including how he sees the world and writes about it.

Your brokenness may be different from mine, but everyone has some broken-ness, many times hidden within the recesses of their hearts.

I don't know *where* you've been broken, but I know God can make you stronger in your broken places. I also know he wants to use your pain as a platform to help others.

I want to be honest: I struggled with including this chapter. It required being vulnerable with the deepest pain of my life. I equate it with running down the street in your boxers (or less.)

I originally cut "A Broken Cup" from this book. When I needed one more chapter so my page count would match the spine width, I realized this was my sign from God to include it. I have a sneaking suspicion it will be the most noteworthy of the sixty-sixty chapters.

I've *fought* depression over the years.

Notice how combat terms are used in describing depression:

"I'm battling depression. "

"It's a *fight."*

"He's gone through *bouts* of depression."

"I've *struggled* with depression."

These descriptive words have a commonality: depression is a great struggle and fierce fight that tests everything within a man or woman.

It's a battle.

That describes my depression. I've battled it.

If I can get as low as I was and bounce back—anyone can. I'm the poster child for hope and healing.

You will get better. Don't give up hope.

Hold onto hope. It's a precious commodity.

Grasp that strong rope called hope.

You're not hopeless. God isn't through with you yet.

You will get better. Don't let go of the rope of hope.

The D-words

There is a list of *D-word*s that travel with depression:

Distortion. Depression is the great liar. It bombards you with lies such as "I'll never get better or regain my happiness and joy."

It tells you so many things that aren't true and clouds everything.

Discouragement. Depression is discouragement that won't go away.

Despair. It's the Biblical word for word for depression, most often used in the Psalms of David.

Darkness. Most depression sufferers use the words such as "darkness, blackness, night." Churchill called his episodes of depression "The Black Dogs."

Dread. There is a loss of joy replaced by fear.

Thoughts of Death. David said it well, "Though I walk through the valley of the shadow of death . . . "Most long-term sufferers experience a wide spectrum of thoughts about death. Few will admit it, but it's part of the illness. Don't listen to those thoughts. You will get better.

Disappointment. "God, I know you can heal me; why don't you do it now?"

Dry. Your soul feels dry. So often, my depressed friends will say that "their soul is dry."

When I'm in deep depression, I'm dry.

I normally *tear up* at the end of "Ol' Yellow," but I have no tears when I'm depressed. I'm dry inside.

Since my mental health has returned, I *tear up* at anything, especially people's hurts and a mockingbird's song. I am not ashamed that my tears come easily. I've got my mental health back, and I am so thankful. Once again, I enjoy people and find joy in the events of life. My creativity has returned, as has my playful sense of humor.

* * *

The best Biblical text on depression is the story of the Prophet Elijah in I Kings 18-19.

In summary, Elijah has come off the greatest victory of his life against King Ahab and his horde of godless prophets. He stands alone and prays down fire from heaven.

Then, he experiences a tremendous letdown: Wicked Queen Jezebel threatens him, and he "is afraid and runs for his life."

After a long, tiring marathon, he goes into the wilderness.

Elijah's burnt out, literally and figuratively.

His tank is dry, and he's depressed.

God seems to be silent. The most painful part of depression is not feeling the presence of God. *He's beside me, but I don't feel it.*

I sense this in Elijah: he's under the broom tree and can't seem to hear God's voice. His prayers seem to be bouncing off the ceiling, or in his case, off the canopy of the broom tree.

I know. You feel that God is a million miles away, even though he's as close as your heartbeat. It's a matter of perception and distortion.

It's hard to pray in that situation. During my darkest days, I had two repetitive prayers:

"Lord, help me."

"Lord, I believe; help my unbelief."

Looking back, I realize those were honest prayers, and God answered both.

Our hero Elijah sits down under a broom tree and prays that he might die.

He laments, "I have had enough, Lord, take my life."

I know the feeling. I've sat under that same broom tree. It's dry and lonely out in the desert. You feel so alone and helpless. "Lord, take my life."

Anyone who has sat under the broom tree for any length of time understands these dark thoughts of death. Ignore them. You will get better. Don't lose hope.

However, in the following passage, God supplies the presence His prophet needs and then provides for his obvious physical needs: rest, food, and water.

Later, when Jesus needed encouragement and prayers as he prepared for the cross, God sent Moses and Elijah, a man who had been broken but still useful.

Sometimes, people ask me, "How can you, *a man of God*, be depressed?'

I simply answer, "Elijah."

A broken man who became stronger in his broken places and continued to be used mightily by God.

Postscript: How did I come out of it?

Finally, I want to share about that strong rope of hope: how I was restored to mental health.

Most of all, my healing came from God, to whom I'm so grateful.

Time. Healing takes time. I didn't get sick overnight, and it took me time to get well.

Support: I've been blessed to have a strong circle of encouragers around me. It begins with my precious wife, DeDe, and extends to my loving family and close friends.

I had several men who walked beside me. I meet another fellow struggler weekly. We help each other.

My best friend James was so faithful and refused to be pushed away. Everyone needs a friend like James Newsom.

I've chosen to be part of a small men's groups who love me, encourage me, and pray for me. Every depressed person needs prayer warriors. My loving church family has stood with me.

I made a decision not to walk this journey alone.

There should be no stigma in seeking help or taking medication. Depression isn't a weakness; it is an illness. We seek medical help for every other sickness; why not depression?

My depression is evidently some type of chemical imbalance. It's simple for me: if I take my meds, I stay healthy; if I don't, I get depressed. Because I know how the bottom feels, I refuse to go off my meds without my doctor's instructions.

Once again, all healing, including all of the above, comes from Jesus, the Great Physician.

Don't lose hope. You will get better. I'm living proof of it.

The Mockingbird's Midnight Song is my memoir of my depression. Because it has helped so many, it's the most satisfying of my fourteen books.

It's available on Amazon and Kindle as an ebook.

Please consider sharing this with anyone who needs this story of hope and encouragement.

Chapter 63

The Mud on My Boots

I walked my property line early this morning after the first killing frost of the year.

The sun was rising through the pines, the ground was covered in a blanket of white, and swirls of fog rose from our pond. I was enveloped in silence, absent from artificial human noises.

In the swamp, I heard a large tree crash to the ground. I wondered about its story. I also smiled: If a tree falls in the middle of the forest with no one there, does it make a noise?

Sure, it does. Just because a human ear doesn't hear doesn't mean anything. When that tree came crashing down, a lizard looked up. A red fox stopped in mid-stride to make note of the fall, and a woodpecker fled off in flight.

As I stood in the silence and solitude of the moment, the world seemed right and in place.

My property is only twelve acres, and the deed says Sidney Curt Iles and DeAnise Terry Iles, but it's ours. I'm Sidney and DeAnise is my wife DeDe. I always laugh that our full names could have come from Downton Abby.

But I'm not sure if we own it.

I recently read a sobering quote: "All property will revert to its original owner."

Yes, "The Earth is the Lord's. . ."

We've finally had several weeks of rain after the long drought of 2023. You can walk through the mud again at the edge of Crooked Bayou Swamp.

I walk the levee of Clayton Iles Pond. It's a special place that we've chosen to name after a remarkable man, my Dad. I notice the water level is the highest it's been in a year.

Daddy gave us the land I'm tracking mud through. He divided forty acres between my two sisters and me, leaving acreage for the house where he and Mom lived.

Daddy had been given this back forty by his grandmother, who'd inherited it from her pioneer parents.

I am once again amazed at the remarkable people I come from. They set the example that although they loved their land, they loved family more.

As I continue walking through the tall grass, I trace small animal trails through the longleaf pines. I check on my trees, which, although planted within two years, range in height from the grassy stage to twenty-foot-tall saplings.

As I've shared throughout my years of writing, the longleaf pine, also known as the yellow pine, is a fascinating tree. Old-timers often called the longleafs "long straw pines."

I walk by one of the grassy stage longleafs. It appears like a clump of grass. I scold it, "Hey, little fellow, you're way behind your brothers and sisters. You'd better get with the program."

The grassy pine doesn't answer. Trees don't talk in spite of what *The Hobbit* says.

Even so, I sense what is happening underground. Even though the straw is short, this tree is putting down a deep tap root into the soil. It's laying a solid foundation for the majestic pine it will one day be. When the right combination of rain, sunshine, and a good woods fire occurs, this small pine will take off and spring up, never again being a prisoner of the weeds and wax myrtles.

It'll spend the rest of its days reaching for the heavens.

It's a great lesson about unseen strength and strong roots.

"My idea of a good time is walking my property line

And knowing the mud on my boots is mine."

—"Property Line"

Toy Caldwell/The Marshall Tucker Band

When I consider the mud on my boots as mine, I'm reminded that I don't own the mud or the land beneath it.

I don't own it, but it definitely owns me.

I've come to realize I'm only a steward of this land—a caretaker. Everything we own comes from the Lord. It's on loan.

Most of all, this land belongs to God. King David, another outdoorsman, said it well in Psalms 24:1, "The earth is the Lord's and the fullness thereof."

As proud as I am of my land and trees, I can't be arrogant. My longleafs, the natural species of much of the Gulf South, are tenacious trees. They thrive on fire, are resistant to bugs, and are impervious to rot. If left alone, they grow majestically to the sky.

But I must remember that the longleafs' greatest enemy is not the crosscut-saw but storms.

Hurricanes wreak havoc on stands of longleaf. My mentor, Mr. Frank Miller, spoke of the aftermath of the Great Storm of 1918, "The tall pines were snapped off like matchsticks."

I know that some future Gulf hurricane could storm through SW Louisiana and leave wreckage and ruin. It's happened twice this century, and it will happen again.

I may be a small-time landowner, but my land and trees are precious.

I'm a farmer—a tree farmer. I am a very small tree farmer, but like generations of men and women connected to the land, I know there is one thing I cannot control: the weather.

It can bless us.

It can destroy us.

Often in the space of the same year.

So, I'm not going to get too puffed up about my trees. I'm only their caretaker. Only their steward.

And I hope they're standing tall when I'm gone.

* * *

Circling back to where we started, I like to think of the mud on my boots as mine, but that's not really true.

First of all, I'm not sure I own it. It seems to own me. It's part of who I am, and I could not separate this land more easily than by cutting off my right arm.

This land owns me.

I can't say I own it. My acreage was given to me as a gift. I didn't buy it; it was given in love. I'm in a line of ancestors who've passed it on hand to hand, heart to heart.

Yes, I don't own this property. I'm simply a steward of it. God has given me squatter's rights for this brief span of my life. I've tried to be a good steward of this land. We've dug a pond, planted pines, erected wood duck boxes, bush-hogged around the borders, and lovingly tended it.

My twelve acres are adjacent to the eighty-acre homestead where the Old House sits. I'm one of eight heirs to it. We are each striving to be good stewards of our homestead.

Yes, I'm not an owner; I'm a steward.

I don't own this land. I'm a caretaker. A tree farmer. A birdwatcher. A walker.

The mud on my boots will one day pass from DeDe and me to our sons. I'm confident they'll be good stewards in their own way and time.

Eventually, they'll pass it on. I have no idea what future generations will do with this land at the end of Clayton Iles Road.

I am filled with pride about this family land that has been passed on to me, but then I realized I only have it on loan.

At some point, someone living in a future that I cannot envision will stand here, looking at the land abstract and wondering who I was.

I don't own this land. It'd be better said that it owns me.

That's not my problem. I leave that in God's hands. He owns it all, anyway.

My job is to enjoy and cherish it.

"Who owns Cross Creek? The red-birds, I think, more than I, for they will have their nests even in the face of delinquent mortgages.

It seems to me that the earth may be borrowed but not bought.

It may be used but not owned.

It gives itself in response to love and tending and offers its seasonal flowering and fruiting. But we are tenants and not possessors, lovers, and not masters.

Cross Creek belongs to the wind and the rain, to the sun and the seasons, to the cosmic secrecy of seed, and beyond all, to time . . ."

—Marjorie Kinnan Rawlings, *Cross Creek.,*

Chapter 64

Remember Where You Came From

"I got too far from my raising,

I forgot where I come from.

And the line between right and wrong was so fine."

—Jason Isbell

"If It Takes a Lifetime"

I t's one of the saddest sentences about a man: "He lost his way."

Let me be clear: women can easily lose their way, too.

It's just that most of the worst crash-and-burns I've seen up close involve men.

Somewhere along the way, they lost their way.

They forgot where they came from.

Regretfully, I've seen it with friends and those I admire. I've also watched in our media-driven world where a celebrity or a politician loses his way.

It doesn't matter if it's royalty or blue-collar: you'll cringe. It's like a roadside car wreck; you want to avert your eyes but can't.

In the Pineywoods, we say, "He lost his way."

As we near the end of *Where I Come From*, it's a good place to stop and talk about not forgetting your upbringing.

I had an old friend who called it "The Sin of the Pineywoods":

Forgetting where you came from and the people who helped you get where you are now.

* * *

A few years ago, I had the privilege of speaking to all of the seniors in the Beauregard Parish School System. I wondered what in the world I would have to say to these students on the cusp of life after school.

I broke it down into three simple points:

Remember where you came from.

You may move to Nashville, Boston, or even Alexandria, but your roots are still deep in the sandy soil of the Louisiana Pineywoods.

Don't forget where you came from, and never be ashamed of your people.

Remember, you didn't get here by yourself.

We're all standing on the tall shoulders of someone else.

Be careful of being born on third base and thinking you hit a triple to get there. Several sacrifice bunts were laid down to get you where you are now.

Be grateful to those who helped you arrive here.

Remember, this is just the beginning of your journey.

Please don't live in the past, but always have a healthy respect for it.

May it be said of you, "She remembered from whence she came."

* * *

You'd enjoy being around my youngest son, Terry. He's a Dry Creek boy with an easy-going smile and one of life's greatest assets: a sense of humor, especially the self-effacing kind.

In third grade, he and several classmates formed the East Beauregard-based *Dawg-World-Order* Wrestling Federation. Terry's wrestling name was T-Dawg.

Principal Tim Cooley banished the D.W.O. from existence at EBHS with the following statement: "I'm in charge of the P.W.O. That's the Paddle-World-Order."

That was warning enough to shut the D.W.O. down.

But even though the Dog-World-Order was history, Terry's nickname stuck: He became The T-Dawg.

Or, more emphatically, The *T-DAWG*.

His lifetime friends still call him that. Even his wife Sara calls him T-Dawg.

Whether he wanted it or not, he's been saddled with T-Dawg.

Not T-Dog.

T-Dawg.

* * *

I raised my three sons to be proud of being from Dry Creek, Louisiana. "Tell people that you're from Dry Creek, Louisiana."

When Terry Iles (T-Dawg to most of us) was accepted at Harvard for his Ph.D., I reminded him that he was entering foreign territory and that they'd make fun of everything about Louisiana.

I told him not to go up there and forget where you're from.

Terry tells the next part of the story best,

"I was in my first Hebrew seminar on Exodus 15. Dr. Levenson had everyone tell where they were from. Most were from major cities.

"I said, 'I'm Terry Iles, and I'm from Louisiana.'

"The classroom went silent.

"Professor Levenson kept asking me for more details until we arrived at Dry Creek as my hometown.

"It became an inside joke for the rest of my time in the program. It came up on a couple of exams and on my comprehensive, too. I remember one of the bonus questions being, 'Explain how there can be *an isles i*n Dry Creek?'

"Everyone had a good time with it, and I laughed along with them."

* * *

Terry has one of life's greatest assets: he can laugh at himself. So he took all of the joking in stride and kept his feet on the ground.

Terry passed that test, but he'd already passed the test that meant the most to his Dad. He never forgot where he came from.

The day Terry graduated from Harvard was a special day for Sara, Terry, and the girls. It took a team effort to get across the line. Terry admits he couldn't have done it without the women in his life. He says that completing a PhD isn't as much about intelligence as it is about perseverance.

It's a marathon, and Terry could not have completed it without Sara, Emma, and Eliza by his side.

* * *

Of course, DeDe and I made our way to Boston for Terry's graduation.

Harvard has many traditions and rites associated with their graduation. When I read about the early morning Commencement procession down Oxford Street, I knew I wasn't going to miss it.

I wanted to see two things: the kilted bagpipers leading the parade and Terry Iles marching in his crimson Harvard robe.

Here they came: a parade of Advanced Degree candidates and graduates marching down Oxford Street to the commencement area, led by a band of kilted bagpipers. I believe they were playing "The Old Spice" jingle.

As the graduates passed in ranks four wide, DeDe and I looked for Terry. At six-feet-four-inches, he's hard to miss.

When we saw Terry, I did what I'd been waiting four years for.

"Way to go, T-Dawg. You made it!"

Then I gave my famous eight-note Dry Creek owl call. It seemed appropriate at the moment.

Terry grinned, shaking his head, as he marched on down Oxford Street.

I wouldn't have missed it for the world.

* * *

He's now *Dr.* T-Dawg.

The man who never forgot where he came from.

It's the mark of a true Pineywoods man.

May it always be so.

Remember where you came from.

"And if you get lost, come on home to Green River."□

—"Green River"

John Fogerty

Chapter 65

A Dry Creek Soldier Comes Home

S aturday, September 7, 2024

Dry Creek, Louisiana

Taps.

Nothing sounds quite like "Taps" echoing off a stand of tall pines.

My friend Randy Sanchez plays "Taps" on a small World War I "Trench Bugle" in the far corner of Dry Creek Cemetery. The antique bugle's unique, raw sound, which no trumpet can replicate, sends a chill through the air.

"Taps" is appropriate because we're bringing a Dry Creek soldier home today.

Andrew Jackson Wagnon will now have a marker beside his wife, Nancy.

We're bringing him home to Dry Creek.

A lost soldier is coming home.

This spot in Dry Creek Cemetery doesn't contain Andrew Jackson Wagnon's remains. He was buried in 1863 in an unmarked grave near Opelousas, Louisiana.

It's only a symbolic granite marker, but I feel in my heart that we're truly bring-ing him home. We're placing a marker by his wife, Nancy. It'll be a testimony that a man named Andrew J. Wagnon walked on this earth.

We're doing the right thing today, and that's what we try to do in the Piney-woods.

The right thing.

The words on the marker are simple and brief, but they tell an uncompleted story:

Lost at War

Andrew J. Wagnon

1824-1863

Co. A Spaight's Batt Tex. C.S.A.

 It's a cool September morning, and a group of thirty Wagnon descendants are clustered around the new marker.

I'm one of them. Andrew Jackson Wagnon and his wife Nancy were my great-great-great grandparents, making me a fifth-generation descendant of these Dry Creek pioneers.

As we stand around this spot, my paternal aunt, JoAnn Iles Edwards, traces the long journey of the Wagnons as they pulled up stakes and left western Georgia, headed to Louisiana's No Man's Land for available free land and elbow room.

She shares of the Wagnons' arrival in Dry Creek about 1855, along with two other Georgia families, the Lyles and Henderson. All three families still have deep roots in the Pineywoods.

Like most men in Dry Creek, Andrew Wagnon joined the Confederate Army. The others came home. He didn't.

That open spot in the cemetery between Nancy Wagnon and her son Jasper has always bothered me. Last year, I stood with Cemetery Board member Larry Singleton and lamented that Andrew Jackson Wagnon didn't have a marker.

Larry went to work. Even after the V.A. turned him down, he kept digging. He's a serious historian and researcher. He was able to track down Andrew's military service in a Texas unit nicknamed "Spaight's Angels," which fought the invading Yankees at Sabine Pass and Calcasieu Pass.

Larry procured the marker, flags, and other items for the dedication. This day would not have happened without Larry Singleton.

Today's dedication ceremony isn't about the Confederacy, nor is it about the Civil War.

It's about a family bringing their Dry Creek soldier home.

It's about time to do this. It's been over one hundred and sixty years since Andrew Jackson Wagnon left Dry Creek for the War, never to return, dying of typhoid fever while encamped near Opelousas, Louisiana.

It's a sobering fact that more Civil War soldiers died of disease than bullets.

* * *

We're placing Andrew's marker beside his wife Nancy, who lived forty-nine years as a war widow until she died in 1912.

Two noteworthy events take place during the ceremony:

Larry Singleton presents a Texas flag to Levi Wagnon, a junior at East Beauregard. Levi, a seventh-generation descendant, represents the Wagnon clan.

Next, we did an unusual thing: we said "The Pledge of Allegiance."

It may seem ironic that we said the pledge at the marker of a rebel soldier who took up arms against the United States.

Here's what I told our family:

"I want you to look around this cemetery. Every person buried here is an American, and that includes Andrew Jackson Wagnon and the fifteen other Confederate veterans buried here. They're all Americans, and we're all Americans."

As I said earlier, today was the right thing to do.

Andrew Jackson Wagnon won't be forgotten in history because we brought a soldier home to Dry Creek.

May he rest in peace.

Chapter 66

I Will Walk With You

W e had a childhood sway-backed horse named "Dan."

Dan would take his time as he ambled through the woods, but when you'd turn him toward the house, Dan would pick up speed to a near-trot.

Ol' Dan was headed for the barn.

My sister Colleen, the queen of puns and pithy sayings, will call home at the end of a trip, "Well, Ol Dan is headed for the barn."

She's on her way home to Dry Creek.

Coming home to Dry Creek. That's a good place to end *Where I Come From.*

We started this journey together, and you've made it to the finish line. I want to thank you for joining me. I don't take it for granted that readers enjoy my stories. I'm still amazed at how folks read my books, and I'm so honored by your presence.

After finishing one of my earlier short story collections, a reader commented, "Well, I guess I now know the *Curt Iles philosophy of life.*"

I'm not sure he meant it as a compliment, but he was right. The sixty-six stories in *Where I Come From* paint a clear picture of my values, beliefs, and background. A part of my life statement is to encourage others. If these stories have heartened you, I am most pleased.

I hope you've discovered the *patterns* strewn along the path and will build some patterns for those to follow.

Maybe even light a signal fire they can follow in the dark.

Leaving this world better than you found it.

Before parting, I'd like to share a final word with you: "Sindikiza."

Sindikiza

Sin-di-kaza.

"I will walk with you." It's a Swahili term that has no comparable English word.

Google Translate states "to escort" for Sindikiza, but that misses the African nuance of the word.

The best translation of Sindikiza is, "I will walk with you."

Here's how it plays out in rural African culture: when you visit the home of an African, they will accompany you all the way from their home to your gate.

I will walk with you. Sindikiza.

Regardless of the distance or weather, your host will walk home with you.

Despite steps,

Nor darkness.

Or rain.

Not even fear of black mambas along the dark path.

I will walk with you.

Not ahead nor behind.

Beside you.

I will walk beside you.

I like the way that sounds: *with you*.

I won't trail behind, nor will I scamper ahead.

I'll walk beside you. You can depend on that.

I related to an African friend, Joseph Anyovi, that we do not have Sindikiza in America. I told him, "Joseph, we Americans leave our guests at the door and quickly lock it behind them. Then, as soon as they pull out of the driveway, we flip the porch light off."

Joseph shook his head, "That is sad, Mzee. That is so sad."

Since returning from Africa, I've tried to adjust Sindikiza to my American lifestyle. I escort guests to their vehicle, wishing them a warm farewell, and wave as they drive off.

I stay outside until their tail lights disappear, then go inside the house, lock the front door, and quickly turn off the porch light.

I think of my friend Joseph. I believe he would be pleased with my weak American attempt at Sindikiza.

Sindikiza. It's a good word, so try it at home.

Sin-di-kiza.

It's a good word to put in your pack for the journey.

It's how I visualize my Jesus. He has walked beside me through the thick and thin, highs and lows. I highly recommend Him as a good partner on your journey.

I will walk with you. Sindikiza.

Now, as they say in Swahili, "Kwheri."

That's goodbye.

Curt Iles

November 2024

Dry Creek, Louisiana

Epilogue

Going Back Down South

"If you want to go,

I'm going to go.

I'm going back down South now."

—"Back Down South"

Kings of Leon

Like me, Mandy comes from a deep line of Pineywoods people. She graduated from East Beauregard High School, the rural school where I served as principal.

After school, Mandy married, started a family, and then moved to the far north country of Michigan. Her husband found good work, and Mandy and her family settled into life in a distant state.

Maybe *settled* is not the best word for it.

During one long northern winter, Mandy's parents, Merlin and Maxine, bundled up a stack of my Creekbank books and mailed them to her.

Later that month, Mandy called home. "Momma, Daddy, we're packing up and coming home. Those Curt Iles books made me homesick, and we're coming South."

I write stories to *move* people, but Mandy's move was on another level.

My stories moved Mandy. It moved her back to the Louisiana Pineywoods.

I recently saw Mandy's parents at a restaurant. Merlin loudly pointed me out, "See that man there? He brought my grandkids back to Louisiana."

I'll probably never receive a *New York Times*-starred review or have my books featured on Oprah, but I'll stack Mandy's review against anything else I get.

I hope that's what *Where I Come From* did for you.

I hope it moved you, too.

To smile, think, even shed a tear or two, care deeper, and love wider.

"The shortest distance between the truth and the human heart is a story."

—Anthony DeMello

Acknowlegements

Friends of Dry Creek

DeDe Iles, Mary Iles, Carolyn and Steve Boniol, Angela Nelson Donovan, Gary and Phyllis Feaster, Frank and Janet Bogard, Paige Bordeon, Frank and Debra Tyler, Julie Johnson, David and Shelly Feaster, Colleen Iles Glaser, Claudia Iles Campbell, Bill Iles, and JoAnn Iles Edwards,

Special Thanks to:

The Paige Thompson clan, Charlie Greg Terry, Andy and Anna Marie Magee, Michael Wynne, Michael Pate, C.W. Johnson, Gary Perkins, Siri, Matheus Alva, Wayne Mullins and the Ugly Mug Crew, Jim Clinton, Bandit Iles, Larry Singleton, Lynn Duck, Quinn Williams, Brenda Brechtel, Jennifer Odom White, Greg Bevels, Anthony Mugisha, and David Brown.

I wrote most of *Where I Come From* at Tamp and Grind Coffee in downtown Alexandria. I'll be forever grateful to Amanda Phillips and the Tamp and Grind Family: Gracie Thompson, Jack Blair, Brooklyn Fisher, Ariel Halfmann, Hannah Lanclos, Madison Ogorek, Morgan Wilkins, Taylor Saucier, Astrid Lemmons, Megan Simmons, Morgan Smith, and Taylor West.

. . . and so many others who helped me bring *Where I Come From* to life.

I always remember that "A book needs friends before it needs readers."

Endnotes

Coming in 2025

A Pineywoods Manifesto: Lessons for Life (Spring 2025)

A Broken Cup: A Journey Through Depression (August 2025)

A Love of the Land   62 new short stories (Late Fall 2025)

__Also by Curt Iles__

Stories from the Creekbank

The Old House

Wind in the Pines

Hearts Across the Water

Deep Roots

The Mockingbird's Midnight Song

Christmas Jelly

The Wayfaring Stranger

A Good Place

As the Crow Flies

A Spent Bullet

Trampled Grass

Uncle Sam: A Horse's Tale

Where I Come From

"Medic!"

Contact: Creekbank Stories

creekbank.stories@gmail.com

www.creekbank.net

About Curt Iles

Curt Iles writes from his homes in Dry Creek, Louisana, and Alexandria, Louisiana.

He is the author of fourteen books celebrating the people, places, and stories of his native Pineywoods.

Curt has been married to DeDe for forty-five years, and they have three sons and nine grandchildren. He is a graduate of Louisiana College and McNeese State University. He has worked as a teacher, coach, principal, camp manager, and missionary.

Curt Iles' Mission Statement

Be a man God can use, be an encourager, and be respected by those who know me best.

Creekbank Stories exists to share moving stories that encourage and inspire.

Learn more at www.creekbank.net

www.ingramcontent.com/pod-product-compliance
Lightning Source LLC
Chambersburg PA
CBHW032117020426
42334CB00016B/990